Published Titles

Concepts in the Social Sciences

Feminism

Jane Freedman

Open University Press
Buckingham · Philadelphia

For Stuart and Olivia

Open University Press
Celtic Court
22 Ballmoor
Buckingham
MK18 1XW

email: enquiries@openup.co.uk
world wide web: www.openup.co.uk

and
325 Chestnut Street
Philadelphia, PA 19106, USA

First Published 2001

A catalogue record of this book is available from the British Library

ISBN 0 335 20415 5 (pb)   0 335 20416 3 (hb)

Library of Congress Cataloging-in-Publication Data
Freedman, Jane.
    Feminism/Jane Freedman.
       p. cm. — (Concepts in the social sciences)
    Includes bibliographical references and index.
    ISBN 0-335-20416-3 — ISBN 0-335-20415-5 (pbk.)
    1. Feminism.   2. Women's rights.   3. Women—Social conditions.
    I. Title. II. Series.

HQ1154.F743 2001
305.42—dc21   00-060679

Typeset by Type Study, Scarborough
Printed in Great Britain by St Edmundsbury Press, Bury St Edmunds

Contents

Introduction: Feminism or Feminisms?

The title of this book should, perhaps, more properly have been *Feminisms,* because, as soon as you attempt to analyse all that has been spoken and written in the name of feminism, it becomes clear that this is not one unitary concept, but instead a diverse and multi-faceted grouping of ideas, and indeed actions. And although many attempts have been made to answer the question 'What is feminism?' with a set of core propositions and beliefs central to all feminist theories, the task is made extremely difficult because many of the different strands of feminism seem to be not only divergent but sometimes forcefully opposed. So, perhaps we should start from the assumption that we cannot define what 'feminism' is, but only try to pick out common characteristics of all the many different 'feminisms'. Any attempt to provide a baseline definition of a common basis of all feminisms may start with the assertion that feminisms concern themselves with women's inferior position in society and with discrimination encountered by women because of their sex. Furthermore, one could argue that all feminists call for changes in the social, economic, political or cultural order, to reduce and eventually overcome this discrimination against women. Beyond these general assertions, however, it is difficult to come up with any other 'common ground' between the different strands of feminism, and as Delmar (1986) argues, one cannot assume that agreement or feminist unity underlies the extreme fragmentation of contemporary feminism. Indeed, such an assumption of underlying unity or coherence of different feminisms may have the unlooked-for effect of marginalizing different groups of women whose concerns fall outside this definition of feminist unity.

If it is difficult (perhaps impossible) to define feminism in terms of a set of core concepts then can feminism be defined better or further in terms of its historical origins and development? The term feminism is a relatively modern one – there are debates over when and where it was first used, but the term 'feminist' seems to have first been used in 1871 in a French medical text to describe a cessation in development of the sexual organs and characteristics in male patients, who were perceived as thus suffering from 'feminization' of their bodies (Fraisse 1995). The term was then picked up by Alexandre Dumas *fils*, a French writer, republican and anti-feminist, who used it in a pamphlet published in 1872 entitled *l'homme-femme*, on the subject of adultery, to describe women behaving in a supposedly masculine way. Thus, as Fraisse (1995: 316) points out, although in medical terminology feminism was used to signify a feminization of men, in political terms it was first used to describe a virilization of women. This type of gender confusion was something that was clearly feared in the nineteenth century, and it can be argued that it is still present in a modified form in today's societies where feminists are sometimes perceived as challenging natural differences between men and women. It is interesting to note, though, that feminist was not at first an adjective used by women to describe themselves or their actions, and one can certainly say that there was what we today would call 'feminist' thought and activity long before the term itself was adopted. In the 1840s the women's rights movement had started to emerge in the United States with the Seneca Falls Convention of 1848 and the resulting Declaration of Sentiments, which claimed for women the principles of liberty and equality expounded in the American Declaration of Independence. This was followed by Elizabeth Cady Stanton and Susan B. Anthony's founding of the National Woman Suffrage Association. In Britain, too, the 1840s onwards saw the emergence of women's suffrage movements. But even before the emergence of organized suffrage movements, women had been writing about the inequalities and injustices in women's social condition and campaigning to change it. In 1792 Mary Wollstonecraft had published *A Vindication of the Rights of Women* and at the same time in France women such as Olympe de Gouges and Théroigne de Méricourt were fighting for the extension of the rights promised by the French Revolution to women. So, although we can trace the development of women's rights movements from the mid-nineteenth century, this was not the starting point for women's concern about their social and political condition.

Feminism is thus a term that emerged long after women started questioning their inferior status and demanding an amelioration in their social position. Even after the word feminism was coined, it was still not adopted as a term of identification by many of those who campaigned for women's rights. Even many of the women's rights organizations in the late 1960s and early 1970s did not call themselves feminist: the term feminism had a restricted use in relation to specific concerns and specific groups (Delmar 1986). It is only more recently that the label feminist has been applied to all women's rights groups indiscriminately, and this non-coincidence between these groups' self-identification and subsequent labelling as feminist clearly relates to the problem of what criteria are to be used in deciding whether a person, group or action is 'feminist'. Should all theories, actions and campaigns that improve women's social position, whether intentionally or not, be classified as feminist? Or must there be a conscious intent to undertake a 'feminist' activity? If the first position is adopted, then it can be argued that the meaning of feminism becomes almost impossibly diffuse. Similarly, there is a query over whether different types of women's political organizing which do not have as a specific goal the furtherance of women's rights – for example, women's peace movements – should be called feminist. Again a positive answer may lead to a diffusion of the meaning of feminist beyond the bounds of what is theoretically or politically helpful. On the other hand, there are those who argue for a much tighter definition of feminism, and, as Delmar (1986: 13) points out:

> There are those who claim that feminism does have a complex of ideas about women, specific to or emanating from feminists. This means that it should be possible to separate out feminism and feminists from the multiplicity of those concerned with women's issues. It is by no means absurd to suggest that you don't have to be a feminist to support women's rights to equal treatment, and that not all those supportive of women's demands are feminists. In this light feminism can claim its own history, its own practices, its own ideas, but feminists can make no claim to an exclusive interest in or copyright over problems affecting women. Feminism can thus be established as a field (and this even if scepticism is still needed in the face of claims or demands for a unified feminism), but cannot claim women as its domain.

In seeking to describe feminism, this book clearly tends towards the position that feminism can claim to be a field with its own ideas, history and practice. It will be stressed throughout the book, however, that these ideas, history and practice are far from unified, and are indeed subject to continuing debate. For practical as well as political purposes, the limits of what feminism is must be drawn at some point, but again we should stress the contested and evolving nature of these boundaries. Thus the ideas and practices described in this book should in no way be understood as a complete and fixed definition of what feminism has meant historically or what it means today.

In an attempt at some kind of classification, histories of feminism have talked about the historical appearance of strong feminist movements at different moments as a series of 'waves'. Thus 'first-wave' feminism is used to refer to the late-nineteenth-century and early-twentieth-century feminist movements that were concerned (although not exclusively) with gaining equal rights for women, particularly the right of suffrage. 'Second-wave' feminism refers to the resurgence of feminist activity in the late 1960s and 1970s, when protest again centred around women's inequality, although this time not only in terms of women's lack of equal political rights but in the areas of family, sexuality and work. This classification is a useful historical summary, but may lead to the false impression that outside these two 'waves' there has been no feminist activity. Certainly, there was less activity that could be called feminist before the suffrage movements at the end of the nineteenth century and the beginning of the twentieth century, but, as argued above, the question of women's social position had been a topic of thought and action well before the word 'feminist' was used. And between the suffrage movement and the reinvigoration of feminism in the late 1960s and 1970s, the issue of women's inequality did not just die away and feminism did not lie dormant, although feminists may have been less visible and their voices heard less during this period. Similarly, the grouping together of feminist movements under a general description of 'first wave' and 'second wave' may act to mask the diversity of feminist thought that has existed both within the two waves and between them, by attempting to give one label to a whole series of different theories and actions. There is thus, for example, a tendency to reduce 'first-wave' feminism to the struggle for suffrage, even though there was a wide divergence of feminist views on women's political rights at the time (as will be discussed further in Chapter 2). So, although it may be true that feminist movements have been more active and have recruited more members at certain historical periods, it would perhaps be more accurate to see feminism not as emerging in 'waves' but as a continuum of thought and action. During the course of this book, therefore, it may be useful to occasionally refer to 'first-wave' and 'second-wave' feminism as terms of description, but it must be remembered that these are used only as terms of convenience and do not intend to convey the idea that feminisms can be easily historically classified into these two periods of activity, or that outside of these periods there was no feminist struggle.

Another problem regarding the classification of feminisms comes where some studies of feminism and feminist theory, rather than take a strictly historical approach, attempt to provide a neat classification of feminism into different theoretical families. A basic version of this categorization would divide feminisms and feminists into three loose groups: liberal feminism, Marxist or socialist feminism, and radical feminism. A brief and rough summary of this typology could be stated as follows: liberal feminists include all those who campaign for equal rights for women within the framework of the liberal state, arguing that the theoretical basis on which this state is built is sound but that the rights and privileges it confers must be extended to women to give them equal citizenship with men; Marxist and socialist feminists link gender inequality and women's oppression to the capitalist system of production and the division of labour consistent with this system; and radical feminists see men's domination of women as the result of the system of patriarchy, which is independent of all other social structures – that is, it is not a product of capitalism. Variations may be introduced depending on how far these classifications consider Marxist and socialist feminism as closely related or separate groupings, or by the introduction of a group of 'dual-systems' feminists, who combine elements of Marxist and radical feminist thinking. More recent surveys have also added on the categories of psychoanalytical feminism, postmodern or poststructuralist feminism, black feminism, and so on. These classifications are undoubtedly useful in providing an intelligible understanding of the positioning of major feminist theorists in relation to each other, and the lucid analyses of feminist theorists and movements provided by writers such as Jaggar (1983), Tong (1992) or Walby (1990), among others, should not be underestimated as an important resource both for students of feminism and for feminists themselves. As with all attempts at classification, however, there seems to be a tendency inherent in this approach to gloss over differences and to prioritize elements of commonality in the various categories of feminism on the one hand, and to emphasize the differences between the categories on the other. Moreover, labels such as liberal, socialist or radical feminist, although adopted by some feminists to describe themselves and their theoretical and practical positions, do not do justice to the complexity of feminism, which is perhaps more aptly described by Nye (1989: 1) as a 'tangled and forbidding web'. This book attempts to untangle this complexity not through a rigid classification of the different feminisms, but through an examination of different issues and problems to which feminists have brought their attentions. This focus on issues and debates may be seen as a more fruitful way of addressing the fragmentation and multiplicity of contemporary feminist debate and of moving beyond a simple oppositional positioning of different strands of feminist thought (Hirsch and Fox Keller 1990). This is, therefore, the approach that this book will adopt, focusing not on the different strands of feminism and feminist thought as such, but exploring the different analyses that various feminists have brought to issues of relevance to women. Again, the nature of this work means that there will not be space in the book to treat all the issues on which feminists have written (ranging from politics, to science, to literature and art and beyond), nor to represent all the multiple feminist voices which have spoken on each issue – to do so would be a mammoth undertaking well beyond the scope of a book such as this. Instead this book aims to tackle some of the major issues that have preoccupied feminists, and to convey some of the principal viewpoints and debates that have arisen in connection with these issues in order to provide the reader with an introduction to some of the key elements of feminist thought. We will thus tackle the issues of women's political participation and citizenship (Chapter 2), their economic situation and their relation to the labour market both nationally and globally (Chapter 3), and issues of sexuality and reproduction (Chapter 4). There is, however, one central question that emerges from feminist debates in all these areas, and that is the question of the meaning of equality for feminism, and more precisely the opposition between 'equality' and 'difference'. As sexual difference has been a constitutive factor in our societies for as long as we can remember, feminists struggling to redefine women's place in society must come up against the problem of how to theorize this difference and how to deal with its consequences in practice. As we will see in Chapter 1, this question has proved central to all the different strands of feminist thought, and the way in which different feminisms have attempted to explain and define sexual difference has had an important impact on their practical applications. With regard to welfare, for example, feminists must ask whether women and men should be treated in exactly the same way, or whether differences should be taken into account when deciding benefits. Furthermore, the question of difference does not just occur in relation to the difference between men and women, but also between women themselves. An assumption among some feminists was that they were speaking about and for all women. However, this assumption is at best optimistic, and at worst an arrogant hegemonic understanding of 'womanhood' – if we take into account the many factors that divide women (factors such as class, race or ethnic identity, age, sexual orientation and so on). When examining feminist theories, we must look carefully, therefore, at what they mean by the use of the category 'women', and at how useful this category may be as a tool of analysis. These issues will be highlighted throughout the book, with Chapter 5 devoted to a discussion of charges of feminist 'essentialism' with regard to the category of women, and the neglect of very real differences among women. In this chapter we will also examine the postmodern and poststructuralist feminist critique of identity politics, and ask if these types of feminist theories provide a way forward for our understanding of difference. The aim of the book is to examine the multiplicity of feminisms and to analyse how their varied approaches can have an impact on the varied lives of women. In doing so, we will seek to be as inclusive as possible of all the feminisms that exist worldwide, but again, the necessarily limited nature of the coverage in this book means that the main focus will be on Western feminisms. Within these limitations, however, the book will attempt to argue that despite the many divergences and conflicts within these feminisms, they all have an important and worthwhile goal which is highly relevant to contemporary society, despite some claims that we have now entered an era of 'post-feminism'. As Lynne Segal (1999: 232) concludes in answer to the question 'why feminism?': 'Because its most radical goal, both personal and collective, has yet to be realized: a world which is a better place not just for some women, but for all women.' And, as she goes on to add, that world would be better not just for women, but for men as well.

1

Equal or Different? The Perennial Feminist Problematic

The debate over equality, its meaning and how or if it may be achieved, and its relevance to women's liberation – a debate that is often referred to in feminist writings as the equality–difference debate – is, as was argued in the introduction, central to feminist analysis and discussion. This equality–difference debate is all the more difficult to overcome as it is a debate whose terms are not easily defined. Put crudely, it is a debate over whether women should struggle to be equal to men or whether they should valorize their differences from men. But the terms equality and difference are themselves contested terms with a multitude of meanings, and so the equality–difference debate is a highly complex one. If women are claiming equality with men, then with which men should they be claiming equality? And on what issues? Should they claim equality of opportunity or equality of outcome? And if women want to valorize their differences, then are these natural, biological differences or differences that are the result of particular social and economic conditions?

These are just a few of the many questions that are provoked by the equality–difference debate and they illustrate why it is such a difficult debate for feminists and why it has led, at times, to a seeming impasse between feminists on opposite sides of the divide. Some have tried to overcome this divide by using postmodernist or poststructuralist critiques to argue that the binary division between equality and difference should itself be deconstructed. This idea (which will be discussed further later in this chapter), or that of a 'third way' between equality and difference, may seem to be attractive in that it promises to rid feminism of one of its perennial conflicts. However, other feminists maintain that the division between equality and difference is one that is here to stay and that in any practical discussion of women's position in society there is no escaping the divide. In discussions on how to treat women's claims for maternity rights, for example, feminists are divided between those who think that maternity benefits should be special rights granted to women on the basis of their specific biological capacity to have children and the particular social role of maternity that they have been assigned in Western societies, whereas others argue that maternity benefits should be subsumed under the general category of sickness benefits so that pregnant women are treated the same as men who have an illness which prevents them from working for a period of time (Bacchi 1991; Bock and Thane 1991).

It is this type of question that leads feminists to argue again over the existence of women's biological and social differences from men and about the best strategies for ending women's subordinate position in society, either through claiming equality or stating their difference. Clearly, this debate is also complicated by differences among women themselves (a question that we will return to in Chapter 5), differences of class, race, age, sexual orientation and so on. And an additional complicating factor in this debate is the fact that women's supposed differences from men have been used over the centuries to justify discrimination against women and their exclusion from full social and political citizenship. Thus, those feminists who argue for difference risk seeming to support the theoretical tools of patriarchal exclusion. As Segal (1987: xii) contends: 'There has always been a danger that in re-valuing our notions of the female and appealing to the experiences of women, we are reinforcing the ideas of sexual polarity which feminism originally aimed to challenge.'

So, what is meant by sexual difference? Feminists have pointed to the way in which, historically, a natural difference between men and women was assumed, and have analysed the ways in which this difference was given various social, political and economic meanings in different societies and civilizations. They argue that one constant of this differentiation, however, has been that women have been given an inferior or secondary status in societies because of this assumed natural sexual difference. As Sherry Ortner (1998: 21) argues: 'The secondary status of woman in society is one of the true universals, a pan-cultural fact.' And as she goes on to explain, this secondary status of women can be explained by the fact that within the multiplicity of cultural conceptions and symbolizations of women that exist and that have existed in different societies, there is a constant in that women are seen as being 'closer to nature' in their physiology, their social role and their psyche. Whereas women have been seen as 'closer to nature', men have been perceived as 'closer to culture', more suited for public roles and political association. For this reason, women have been relegated to a secondary status in society, often confined to roles in the home rather than able to accede to powerful public positions. It is understandable, then, that, as soon as feminists began to campaign against women's secondary social status, they began to question the assumed natural differences between men and women, and the consequences of these assumed differences on social organization. The question then arose of how to challenge this assumption of difference. Should women deny sexual difference and claim equal rights on the basis that they are the same as men? Or should they, on the other hand, argue that they are equal but different, and that their specific 'feminine' qualities are as valuable and as important as 'masculine' attributes. This equality–difference debate is one that has remained central to feminism, and has become even more complex and varied with modern social and scientific developments. The development of effective means of contraception and of new reproductive technologies, for example, has meant that women are no longer tied to the biological function of reproduction in the same way as they once were, and for some this may signify the opening up of new possibilities for the attainment of 'equality'.

Despite the huge social changes that have taken place in the past century, however, the concept of difference between men and women still prevails in society. A key problem that feminists identify in this continuing perception of difference is that it is almost impossible to escape the formation of social hierarchies based on these perceptions and representations of difference. In fact, feminists argue, the idea of difference is never neutral in its effects on social structures. Contemporary social policy and the structuring of welfare, for example, involve discussions about whether men and women should be treated identically with respect to benefits or whether relevant differences should be taken into account. Although some people argue that men and women are equal but different, it seems impossible to argue for difference without creating some kind of hierarchy. Feminists have, therefore, had to develop different strategies to cope with this question of difference: either denying it, or emphasizing it and giving it a positive value. As Hester Eisenstein and Alice Jardine remark in the introduction to their book *The Future of Difference* (1988: xxv, original emphasis):

> Western culture has proven to be incapable of thinking not-the-same without assigning one of the terms a positive value and the other, a negative. The response to difference on the part of women varies: there are those who exalt it by embracing a certain biology – and a certain eroticism. There are also those who deny it, or, rather, who seek to defuse the power of difference by minimising biology and emphasising cultural coding: on some level, these responses are saying, 'Woman would be the same as ... if only.' A third strand states, like the first group, that women are indeed different from men, but for feminist reasons they add: women are also *better* than men. This group's reasons would not be biological but sociocultural: as outsiders and nurturers, women do things differently from, and better than, men.

This debate over equality and difference has been couched in various terms over the history of feminist activism. Ann Snitow poses the question as a tension between 'needing to act as a woman and needing an identity not overdetermined by gender' (1990: 9). She then goes on to describe the way this tension has been theorized as a divide between 'minimizers' and 'maximizers' (where the minimizers are those who wish to undermine the category of women by minimizing the difference between men and women, and the maximizers are those who wish to reclaim the category of women and revalue it in order to empower women); between radical feminists and cultural feminists; between essentialists and social constructionists; between cultural feminists and poststructuralists; and between motherists and feminists. What is clear in all this is that although the labels used to define the two sides of the debate may have changed over time and in different societies, the basic tension remains. Moreover, this divide does not cut neatly between different feminist groupings, with the split reappearing in the categories

of radical feminism, cultural feminism, poststructuralist feminism
and so on. As Snitow (1990: 17) argues, this divide is fundamental
at various levels of analysis – material, psychological, linguistic:

> For example, US feminist theorists don't agree about whether post-
> structuralism tends more often toward its own version of essentialism
> (strengthening the arguments of maximizers by recognizing an endur-
> ing position of female Other) or whether poststructuralism is instead
> the best tool minimalists have (weakening any universalized, perma-
> nent concept such as Woman). Certainly poststructuralists disagree
> among themselves, and this debate around and inside poststructural-
> ism should be no surprise. In feminist discourse a tension keeps form-
> ing between finding a useful lever in female identity and seeing that
> identity as hopelessly compromised.

Here we find the heart of the problem for feminists: in trying to fight
for women's emancipation and for 'equality' for women (however
that equality is defined), feminists identify women as a specific
social group with a collective identity that forms a basis for struggle.
In pointing to a collective identity among women, however – an
identity that is different from that of men – feminists risk reproducing, albeit in differing forms, the definitions of difference that
have kept women subordinated for so long.

The biology debate: sex and gender

One central factor in this equality–difference debate is the question
of the relevance of biological differences between men and women.
For centuries, biological difference has been the starting point and
justification for the creation of different social roles for women and
men. Not only was women's biological capacity for childbirth and
breastfeeding and their generally lesser physical strength seen as
determining their social role in the home, occupying themselves
with domestic chores and bringing up children, but it was also
claimed that these biological differences made them unfit to participate in the public sphere. Women were judged to be less reason-
able than men, more ruled by emotion, and thus incapable of
political decision-making, for example. These types of assertions by
philosophers and political theorists were supported by anatomists
and biologists who, as scientific knowledge of the human body
advanced in the nineteenth and twentieth centuries, began to use
data such as measurements of brain size to establish a difference in
intelligence between men and women. Although this crude type of

scientific differentiation between men and women is now almost universally acknowledged as worthless, there is a continuing attempt to provide empirical scientific data to support the idea of innate biological differences between men and women. As Lynne Segal (1999) points out, the late 1980s and 1990s saw a resurgence of social Darwinism, scientific theories that seek to explain male and female behaviour in terms of the demands of human evolution and survival, and that therefore dismiss the idea that masculinity and femininity are social constructs in favour of purely biological explanations. Segal (1999: 82) quotes, for example, the scientist Robert Wright, who she says:

> throughout the 1990s has consistently ridiculed feminists seeking equality with men as doomed by their deliberate ignorance or foolish denial of the 'harsh Darwinian truths' about human nature ... As Wright likes to reassure himself and the many readers of his best-seller *The Moral Animal: Why We Are the Way We Are*, feminists have managed to procure legislation against sexual harassment, and even elements of affirmative action for women, but they will never share power with men because they lack men's genes for competitiveness and risk-taking behaviour.

Faced with this supposedly scientific justification for women's exclusion from large areas of social participation, feminists began to question the link between different physiological characteristics and a 'natural' differentiation in social roles for men and women, and began to formulate ways of overcoming it. For many feminists this has involved a denial of the relevance of biological differences between men and women for the organization of society. This has led to a distinction in much feminist theory between physiological 'sex' and social 'gender'. This distinction can also be expressed by the terms 'female' and 'feminine', 'female' being the biological category to which women belong and 'feminine' behaviour and roles being the social constructions based on this biological category. Thus, many feminists have argued that whereas biological sex is a 'naturally' occurring difference, all the roles and forms of behaviour associated with being a woman have been created historically by different societies.

This distinction between biological sex and social gender is clearly present, although it is not made explicitly in those terms, in a book that has had an important influence on feminist thought, Simone de Beauvoir's *Le Deuxième Sexe* (The Second Sex) (1949). De Beauvoir's famous assertion that 'one is not born a woman: one

becomes one' encapsulates an argument that women's inferior position is not a 'natural' or biological fact but one that is created by
society. One may be born as a 'female' of the human race but it is
civilization which creates 'woman', which defines what is 'feminine', and proscribes how women should and do behave. And what
is important is that this social construction of 'woman' has meant a
continued oppression of women. The social roles and modes of
behaviour that civilizations have assigned to women have kept
them in an inferior position to that of men. This means that women
are not like the working classes in Marxist ideology: they have not
emerged as an oppressed group because of particular historical
circumstances, but have always been oppressed in all forms of social
organization. De Beauvoir does not, however, argue that there is
no biological distinction to be made between men and women.
Although she maintains that the psychological and behavioural
aspects of 'sex' are the products of patriarchal cultures and not the
inevitable products of biological differences, she argues that there
is an irreducible biological difference between men and women.
Woman is a biological and not a socio-historical category, even
though all the behaviour associated with femininity is clearly a
social construction. The liberation of women thus depends on
freeing women from this social construct of the 'eternal feminine',
which has reduced them to a position of social and economic infe-
riority, but it does not depend on the denial of 'men' and 'women'
as biologically distinct categories. As she argues (1949: 13):

> To refuse the notions of the eternal feminine, the Black soul, the
> Jewish character, is not to deny that there are today Jews, Blacks,
> women: such a denial does not represent for the interested parties a
> liberation, but rather an inauthentic flight. It is clear that no woman
> can claim, without bad faith, to be above her sex.

De Beauvoir's distinction between biological sex and the social
creation of the 'eternal feminine' is a precursor of the distinction
between sex and gender that is common in much feminist theory. As
Ann Oakley (1997) explains, the term gender originated in medical
and psychiatric usage where, from the 1930s, psychologists used the
word gender to describe people's psychological attributes without
linking these to men and women. In 1968, Robert Stoller, a psychia-
trist, published *Sex and Gender* – a book about how children who
were biologically (according to chromosomes) of one sex seemed to
belong to the other sex. Most commonly found were babies who

were genetically female but who were born with male external genitalia – these babies could be brought up as either male or female and would develop the 'appropriate gender identity'. Gender was thus used by Stoller to refer to behaviour, feelings, thoughts and fantasies that were related to the sexes but that did not have primary biological connotations (cited in Oakley 1997: 31). This use of gender to refer to attributes that are related to the division between the sexes but are not primarily biologically determined was adopted by feminists to separate innate biological differences between men and women, and socially constructed differences. Oakley, for example, made a distinction between sex and gender in her book *Sex, Gender and Society*, first published in 1972, and argued that:

> 'Sex' is a word that refers to the biological differences between male and female: the visible difference in genitalia, the related difference in procreative function. 'Gender', however, is a matter of culture: it refers to the social classification into 'masculine' and 'feminine'.
>
> (Oakley 1972: 16)

The use of gender, and more specifically the distinction between sex and gender, as a tool of analysis has clearly helped feminist theory to advance on the question of difference, separating the biological from the social and arguing that the two are distinct categories. This has enabled feminists to argue against biological determinism of all kinds and to move the emphasis away from physiological differences between men and women and on to the social processes that shape masculinity and femininity. This process of social construction was a principal focus for many classic feminist texts of the 1970s and 1980s, as Oakley (1997: 33) explains:

> Many classics of feminist writing during this period are hard-hitting elaborations on the basic theme of social construction; society, psychology, sociology, literature, medicine, science, all 'construct' women differently, slipping cultural rhetoric in under the heading of biological fact. It is cultural prescription – gender, not sex – which explains why women fail to have proper orgasms, are ill-fitted to be brain surgeons, suffer from depressive illness, cannot reach the literary heights of Shakespeare, and so on and so forth ... During this period, even/especially influential theories such as Freud's about the origins of 'sexual' difference came to be restated in the language of 'gender development'.

Thus the concept of gender seemed to open up whole new avenues of thought and analysis for feminists, bringing with it the hope of huge theoretical advances in the analysis of women's oppression. As Christine Delphy (1996: 33) argues, the arrival of the concept of gender made possible three linked advances: all the differences between the sexes which seemed to be social and arbitrary, whether they actually varied from one society to another or were just held to be susceptible to change, were gathered together in one concept; the use of the singular term (gender) rather than the plural (sexes) meant that the accent was moved from the two divided parts to the principle of partition itself, and feminists could focus on the way in which this partition was constructed and enforced; and finally, the concept of gender allowed room for an idea of hierarchy and power relations, which meant that the division could be considered from another angle.

However, despite the many advantages that the use of the concept of gender and the theoretical separation between gender and biological sex have provided for feminists, gender is still a problematic term that seems to have lost some of the 'revolutionary' potential it once possessed as it has become accepted into common usage: 'Today, gender slips uneasily between being merely another word for sex and being a contested political term' (Oakley 1997: 30). One of the difficulties has been that, although, as Delphy (1996) argued, the concept of gender opens up the possibility of an analysis of hierarchy, gender analysis may lead to the neglect of the power inequalities that exist between men and women. Talking about men and women as 'engendered', with the implication that both masculinity and femininity are social constructs, may in fact suggest difference rather than power inequality (Oakley 1997). Furthermore, gender is sometimes seen as something that is relevant only to women – because gender was so readily adopted by feminists to explain women's subordinate position in society, it may be perceived as a term that applies only to women and the social construction of femininity (although there seems to have been a recent upturn in academic studies of masculinity). Oakley points out that gender is a term that has been used by academic feminists to bring respectability to their work – talking about 'gender' rather than about 'women' – because the study of women is not really respectable. She comments (1997: 30) that: 'Such a strategy only works because gender was invented to help explain women's position: men neither wonder about theirs nor need to explain it.' The fact that only women seem to have gender clearly demonstrates the operation of power inequalities,

but these inequalities are sometimes overlooked, or their operation is not fully explained merely by an analysis of how gender is
constructed.

Perhaps even more importantly, the very distinction between sex
and gender, and the relationship between the two terms, have been
called into question. Critics argue that the distinction between sex
and gender often leads to a failure to interrogate the nature of sex
itself. Gender is seen as the content, with sex as the container
(Delphy 1996: 33), and although gender is perceived as variable, the
'container' of sex is perceived to be universal and unchanging
because it is 'natural'. In other words, the distinction between sex
and gender means that there is a failure to call into question the
ways in which society constructs 'sex' – that is, the 'natural' body
itself. Sex is seen as a primary division on which gender is predi-
cated. In response, some feminists have argued against this seemingly natural precedence of sex before gender and have argued that
biological sex itself is a social construct – that biology is not
'natural' and universal, but is also, like gender, socially mediated.
In his historical study of the construction and representation of sex,
Thomas Laqueur (1990) points out the way in which up until the
end of the seventeenth century male and female bodies were not
conceptualized in terms of difference; instead, testicles and ovaries,
for example, were seen as equivalent and indeed shared the same
name. It was only in the eighteenth century that sexual difference
was 'discovered'. Similarly, it has been pointed out that, for biologists, sex is composed of a number of different indicators which all
have a varying correlation with one another, and the reduction of
these various elements to one indicator of division (such as the possession or non-possession of a penis) is clearly a social act (Hurtig
and Pichevin 1986). This type of analysis clearly destabilizes the
division btween sex and gender and has led some feminists such as
Delphy (1996) to argue that in fact gender precedes sex. From
another angle, Judith Butler (1990) has attempted to deconstruct
the sex/gender distinction along with other binary distinctions such
as that between nature and culture, and so on.

For some feminists, the need to emphasize the social construction of sex has led to a rejection of gender as a term that is not only
unnecessary but that also leads to confusion because the use of
gender to describe something that is socially constructed implies
that biological sex itself is natural. Monique Wittig, for example,
maintains that sex is nothing more than a social construct and that

the division between men and women is merely a product of social power relations with no basis in nature or human biology.

> There is no sex. There is but a sex that is oppressed and sex that oppresses. It is oppression that creates sex and not the contrary. The contrary would be to say that sex creates oppression, or to say that the cause (origin) of oppression is to be found in sex itself, in a natural division of the sexes pre-existing (or outside of) society.
>
> (Wittig 1996: 25)

According to Wittig, therefore, women are nothing more than an oppressed social class. The disappearance of oppression and therefore of the dominant and the dominated (the 'sex class' of men and that of women) will see the elimination of women and of men as distinct groups of human beings. In this world where sex classes will no longer exist, freedom for all human beings will be attained 'beyond the categories of sex', and both the concept and the real existence of men and women will give way to the 'advent of individual subjects' (Wittig 1996: 20).

These criticisms of gender and of the binary divide between gender and sex do seem to have some foundation. The use of gender can mean that power is evacuated from the analysis of relationships between men and women, and that agency is denied both to women and men (if masculinity and femininity, dominance and oppression are social constructs, then what place is left for the individual agent?). Moreover, as various feminist writers have emphasized, any binary division that sees sex as natural and gender as socially constructed must be avoided. Having said this, however, it may be argued that there is still some power in the use of gender as a term of analysis and that one of the tasks of contemporary feminism should be to try to clarify the complex relationships between gender, sex and power that pervade our society.

Returning to difference: morality, mothering and an ethic of care

The distinction between sex and gender was first used by feminists to move the focus away from supposedly 'natural' and universal differences between men and women and to put the emphasis on the way in which society created these differences. Whether talking in terms of sex or gender, however, differences do still clearly exist and there have been a variety of feminist responses to deal with this: whether to minimize the relevance of difference and to claim that men and women should be treated alike, or to insist that differences do matter and even to valorize these differences.

One facet of sexual difference that has been explored by feminists is that of women's different moral stance. Much of this work was undertaken in response to Freud's claims of a biologically determined sexual difference in morality. Freud's claims about women's weaker moral development have led feminist psychologists and psychoanalysts to explore this area of difference and to ask whether women and men do have a differentiated moral development and if so what causes this and what are its consequences. A famous example of this type of analysis is Carol Gilligan's study *In a Different Voice* (1982), in which she challenges the sexism implicit in many psychological studies of moral development – a sexism that takes male moral development as the norm for human moral development and thus does not recognize women's conceptions of morality as equally valid. More specifically, Gilligan argues against the notion that women have a less developed sense of morality and claims instead that women have a different sense of morality from men. In other words, whereas men's moral thinking depends more on notions of justice, women's morality is more relational and focused more around an ethic of care. Gilligan's study was based primarily on the moral views of women who were deciding whether to have an abortion, and she discovered that these women had a conception of the self that was different from that of most men. Women saw themselves as connected to others and dependent on others for their identity rather than autonomous and separate, as men tend to see themselves. This differing conception of self leads, Gilligan argues, to differences in the ways in which women and men make moral decisions. Women, she claims, tend to emphasize relationships to others and to give these priority over abstract rights; they are more mindful of the consequences of an action rather than just the principles by which the action may be judged right or wrong; and women tend to interpret moral choices in the particular context in which they are made rather than judging them hypothetically or in an abstract fashion. Women's moral 'voice' has gone unheard for so long because their way of making moral judgements is deemed inferior to that of men, whose 'voice' is taken as the norm.

Gilligan has been accused of essentialism in her work – in other words, of positing a natural, universal and essential difference between men and women. She does, however, stress that she sees the difference in men and women's moral stance as a product not of some innate biological essence, but as arising in a social context where factors of social status and power combine with reproductive biology to shape the experiences of men and women and the relationships between the sexes. The criticism of essentialism often comes from those who are fearful that any work claiming to have discovered a difference between men and women in moral terms risks providing ammunition for those who wish to claim that natural and essential differences mean that men and women can never be 'equal'. Critics also argue that the female 'ethic of care' that Gilligan describes is something that has been developed as a strategy for coping and survival in male-dominated societies; why should this 'survival strategy' be celebrated as an achievement of female character and values? On the other hand, there are many feminists who have found Gilligan's work inspiring in the way that it undermines the assumptions not only of traditional psychology and psychoanalytic theory, but also of classic moral and political philosophy. Seyla Benhabib (1988), for example, argues in Gilligan's favour and states that her work forms part of a vital feminist challenge to the presuppositions of traditional moral philosophy, which makes universalist claims on the basis of what she calls the 'generalized other' – the citizen or individual of traditional moral and political thought, who is supposedly an individual with no specific defining characteristics. This 'generalized other' is meant to be gender neutral, but because the philosophies and modes of thought based on this universal generalized other have been formulated by men, they are often alien to women. For Benhabib, Gilligan's work has highlighted the ways in which women have been left out and alienated by male ways of posing moral dilemmas, and has emphasized the need to take account of the 'concrete' other (the other who has specific characteristics and relationships) when making moral judgements:

> What Carol Gilligan has heard are those mutterings, protestations and objections that women, confronted with ways of posing moral dilemmas that seemed alien to them, have voiced. Only if we can understand why their voice has been silenced, and how the dominant ideals of moral autonomy in our culture, as well as the privileged definition of the moral sphere, continue to silence women's voices, do we have a hope of moving to a more integrated vision of ourselves and of our fellow humans as generalized as well as 'concrete' others.
>
> (Benhabib 1988: 95)

Thus, feminist psychologists such as Gilligan have argued that women do have different moral standpoints, and that acknowledging these differences and incorporating women's different approach into our moral and political schemata is important. This argument in favour of difference is perceived by some feminists as dangerous, as it reinforces the idea of a separation between the sexes and so hampers women's quest for equality. Others believe that it is important to express such differences and to give back value to the 'feminine' values that have been denied their true place by the male definition of the norms of morality. However, for those who agree that women do have a different moral standpoint, a further question is how this difference develops. Although some feminists have suggested that innate biological differences between men and women lead to differing moral viewpoints, others point to social factors that influence men and women's development in varying ways. One of the key issues discussed in this regard is women's role as mothers.

Most feminists have pointed to the ways in which women's physical ability to produce children has had some influence on their social position. Although for some, like Shulamith Firestone (1979), it is this biological capacity to reproduce that is the key to women's oppression; for others, this capacity and the social roles and skills which it entails contain some valuable elements that constitute the core of women's difference from men. Mothering is not only about biological reproduction but about a set of attitudes, skills and values that accompany it, and some feminists argue that it is these attitudes, values and skills which constitute the distinctness of femininity and which should be given a more central place in our societies.

We will discuss feminist arguments over reproduction and mothering further in Chapter 4, but it is important to mention the debate over mothering in any discussion of difference because, for many, mothering is the key to men and women's difference. If mothering is seen as central to the difference between men and women, it is then vital to explain why women mother. This is the subject tackled by Nancy Chodorow in her book *The Reproduction of Mothering* (1978). Chodorow sets out to explore why women choose to mother. She rejects the idea that mothering is an innate, natural instinct, and equally the idea that it is merely the result of social conditioning, for, as she argues, this would imply that women had a free choice in the matter of whether to mother.

Instead, by the time people are old enough to make any kind of rational choice, there is already a clear gender difference and a splitting of roles between women who mother and men who do not. Chodorow argues that the desire to mother is part of the desire to be feminine, which girls pick up at an early age. In fact, this happens so young that it cannot be part of a conscious choice but must be mainly an unconscious choice. The sexual and familial division of labour in which women mother and are more involved in interpersonal and affective relationships than men are, leads to a division of psychological capacities in daughters and sons. Because of this division of psychological capacities, these daughters and sons then go on to reproduce the sexual and familial division of labour of their parents. The reproduction of mothering begins from the earliest mother/infant relationship in the pre-Oedipal stage of development. The daughter's sense of self and of gender is identified with her mother, whereas the son feels the need to break the attachment to his mother. This differing psychosexual development means that boys grow up with an ability to relate deeply to others but with more of the single-minded, competitive values that are necessary for success in public life, whereas girls grow up to reproduce their mother's capacity to relate to others, to nurture, and to mother. These qualities of mothering have been undervalued in the public sphere, but Chodorow argues that if both men and women mothered equally, then girls and boys would not grow up with these different qualities; men would be more loving and connected to others, and women would be more autonomous and competitive.

This solution of 'dual-parenting' and for sharing the roles and values of mothering between men and women has, like Gilligan's argument for promoting an ethic of care, been criticized by other feminists. Those who disagree with Chodorow argue that, apart from focusing on white middle-class families and thus falling into the trap of ethnocentrism, her theory centres too closely on the psychosexual workings of the family and ignores or underestimates wider social forces. But as Rosemarie Tong argues, despite the drawbacks evident in both Chodorow and Gilligan's analyses, they, like other feminists who have looked for the roots of difference in women and men's psychological development, have picked out issues which 'mesh with many of our ordinary intuitions about sexual behaviour, mothering and moral conduct' (1992: 171).

Beyond the equality–difference debate?

This chapter has highlighted some of the many ways in which feminists have talked about difference, and the means with which they have tried to overcome traditional views of sexual difference in order to promote women's emancipation. For some, the whole equality–difference debate is now one that does more harm than good to the feminist cause. Joan Scott, for example, argues that the two opposing poles of equality and difference have been fixed in a binary opposition and that this opposition is one of those that feminists must deconstruct:

> Instead of framing analyses and strategies as if such binary pairs were timeless and true, we need to ask how the dichotomous pairing of equality and difference itself works. Instead of remaining within the terms of existing political discourse, we need to subject those terms to critical examination. Until we understand how the concepts work to constrain and construct specific meanings, we cannot make them work for us.
>
> (1990: 139)

Scott's argument for the deconstruction of the binary opposition between equality and difference is convincing if we understand this division as that between an argument that women are the same as men and an argument that they are different. This type of crudely formulated opposition works to suppress the recognition of differences within the categories of women and men and to gloss over the ways that the differences between men and women have been perceived and represented over time and in various societies. It seems, though, that, however hard feminists try to move beyond equality and difference, the questions raised by this debate recur time and again, albeit in varying formulations. For example, I have previously mentioned the debate over maternity provision and whether this should be considered as a different and specific benefit for women or as the same as any other sickness benefit for men and women. This perhaps is what makes the equality–difference debate so resistant – its continually changing formulation. Moreover, it seems that, over time, those who were on one side of the debate may move to the other, and vice versa. Feminists may even find themselves split between varying positions when debating different issues. And although Scott and others see the ongoing debate as somehow harmful to the feminist cause, diverting attention away from the real issues, perhaps it is time to view this debate as something which is in fact valuable and which forces feminists to interrogate themselves as to where they stand in relation to particular issues. Equality–difference must not be perceived as a debate whose terms are fixed in stone, and a debate on which one has always to take the same side; I would argue that feminists will always, in one way or another, be talking about issues in terms of equality and difference, and that this debate may in fact prove positive in many cases. As Anne Snitow (1990: 31) remarks:

> If the divide is central to feminist history, feminists need to recognize it with more suppleness, but this enlarged perspective doesn't let one out of having to choose a position in the divide. On the contrary, by arguing that there is no imminent resolution, I hope to throw each reader back on the necessity of finding where her own work falls and of assessing how powerful that political decision is as a tool for undermining the dense, deeply embedded oppression of women. By writing of the varied vocabularies and constructions feminists have used to describe the divide, I do not mean to intimate that they are all one, but to emphasize their difference. Each issue calls forth a new configuration, a new version of the spectrum of feminist opinion, and most require an internal as well as external struggle about goals and tactics. Though it is understandable that we dream of peace among feminists, that we resist in sisterhood the factionalism that has so often disappointed us in brotherhood, still we must carry on the argument among ourselves. Better, we must actively embrace it. The tension in the divide, far from being our enemy, is a dynamic force that links very different women. Feminism encompasses central dilemmas in modern experience, mysteries of identity that get full expression in its debates. The electricity of its internal disagreements is part of feminism's continuing power to shock and involve large numbers of people in a public conversation far beyond the movement itself. The dynamic feminist divide is about difference; it dramatizes women's differences from each other – and the necessity of our sometimes making common cause.

In the following chapters we will aim to demonstrate the way feminists have been divided over issues relating to equality and difference, and also the ways in which their unity has brought change in some areas which are vital to women's lives.

2

Feminism and the Political: The Fight for Women's Citizenship

Although feminism can be seen as a highly political movement in its attempts to define oppressions and effect social change, feminist relationships to 'the political', if we take this to mean the traditionally defined formal sphere of politics, have been complex and difficult. On the one hand, feminists have sought to end women's continuing exclusion from formal state political institutions and sites of political power, whereas on the other hand, they have argued that the theoretical bases on which these institutions are established are flawed, and further, that the definition of the political must be extended beyond the institutions and issues to which it has traditionally been limited – to include, for example, the family and personal relationships. This chapter will examine feminist critiques of and its relationship to the political, first examining feminist analyses of women's exclusion from formal politics, and then going on to consider different feminist definitions of 'the political' and to analyse ways in which feminists have sought to attain full political citizenship for women.

The starting point for many feminist analyses of politics has been the fact that women have been excluded from the exercise of political power. For long periods of history women were denied the vote in Western democracies, and women are still dramatically under-represented in formal political institutions and decision-making bodies worldwide. Thus, it can be convincingly argued that politics (or at least formal politics) has been, and continues to be, a masculine-dominated activity. As Brown (1988: 4) argues:

> More than any other kind of human activity, politics has historically borne an explicitly masculine identity. It has been more exclusively limited to men than any other realm of endeavour and has been more intensely, self-consciously masculine than most other social practices.

European and American feminists have traced women's political exclusion to the very roots of Western political theories and institutions, analysing the ways in which Western democratic institutions have historically excluded women from access to full political citizenship and political power. For centuries, women were denied the right to vote or to participate in political decision-making in other ways, as they were deemed too irrational to share in political power with men. Political theorists and philosophers, from Plato and Aristotle to Hobbes, Locke and Rousseau, argued for a natural difference between men and women; men being naturally more rational and therefore suited to politics and public life, and 'irrational' women being more suited to the emotional life of the home. Although these arguments that classify women as naturally unfit for political power have been diminished or modified, feminists today point to women's continuing exclusion from full political citizenship, an exclusion that can be traced to underlying assumptions about women's proper role in society, and to the continuing masculine domination of structures of power. In searching for the bases of women's exclusion from the political sphere, feminist theorists have criticized the theoretical bases on which Western democratic institutions are built, in particular the division between public and private, which lies at the heart of both liberal and republican theories and the construction of the individual citizen in these two traditions.

The public and the private

Both liberal and republican traditions have relied on a central division between the public and the private sphere. In the liberal tradition the private sphere is seen as an area of individual freedom, where man is unconstrained by the power of the state, whereas in the republican tradition it is the public sphere that is seen as the domain of true freedom, for there man realizes his true humanity through active citizenship and participation. In both these traditions, however, women have been relegated to the private sphere of life – to the family, where it is assumed that they have their proper place – and this sphere of private/family life has been perceived as outside the concerns of the law-makers in the public realm.

A central feminist critique of liberal contract theory is that of Pateman (1988), who argues that theorists talking about the social contract have ignored the sexual contract, which is the basis of women's subordination. Both men's freedom and women's subjection, she argues, are created through the original contract, with the resulting civil freedom being a masculine attribute depending on patriarchal right. Women, who are assumed to lack naturally the attributes and capacities of 'individuals', are denied this civil freedom. Sexual difference therefore signifies political difference, the difference between freedom and subjection. The private sphere is typically presumed to be a necessary and natural foundation for civil or public life, but at the same time is treated as irrelevant to the concerns of political theorists and political activists. This is still true in modern liberal contract theory (such as that of Rawls) where a natural separation is assumed between public and private, although feminists have argued for the interdependence of the two spheres. Thus, to try to overcome women's subordination and ensure full political citizenship merely by claiming that the individual treated by the social contract is gender neutral, and that the rights bestowed by this contract apply equally to all, is not an adequate response, ignoring as it does the interrelation between civil (public) and private spheres:

> To argue that patriarchy is best confronted by endeavouring to render sexual difference politically irrelevant is to accept the view that the civil (public) realm and the 'individual' are uncontaminated by patriarchal subordination. Patriarchy is then seen as a private familial problem that can be overcome if public laws and policies treat women as if they were exactly the same as men.
>
> (Pateman 1988: 17)

Fraisse (1995) provides a similar critique of French republican thought. Although women participated actively in the French Revolution, the post-revolutionary regime excluded them from full political citizenship. Fraisse describes three axes of exclusion that can be traced in post-revolutionary theory: democratic thought, which excluded women from citizenship; republican thought, which excluded women from representation; and feudal or monarchical thought, which ensured the continuing symbolic representation of political power as masculine. The crucial point in these debates was the question of sexual difference. As she explains, democracy is a question not just of equality but of identity – the identity of the individual who is admitted to full citizenship. Democratic theorists were afraid that real equality between the sexes would efface the necessary distinction between men and women and would lead to confusion between the masculine and the feminine. This equality between the sexes would lead to friendship replacing love and would destroy sexual relations. Thus, it was important to maintain the boundaries of sexual difference, and to incorporate this difference in the new democratic equality. 'The exclusion of women at the birth of democracy was a response to the profound anxiety of men, that of no longer finding in women the other to themselves, the other who assured their power' (Fraisse 1995: 330). Added to this refusal in democratic theory of true equality between men and women was the republican insistence on the separation between the public and the private spheres, a separation that was clearly made along the lines of gender. As Rousseau argued, women were the 'precious half of the Republic'; they made the customs while the men made the laws. Thus, women should limit themselves to domestic government and not mix themselves in the public space of politics.

In exposing the exclusion of women from the political world, feminists pointed out the arbitrary and false nature of the boundaries that had been drawn between the private and public spheres, and argued that true equality could not be achieved by just 'adding in' women to traditional political theories, but that the very basis of these theories must be challenged. Criticisms of the division between public and private in Western political thought led 'second-wave' feminists in the 1960s and 1970s to declare that 'the personal is political', challenging traditional views on the family and personal life as outside the remit of 'politics', and arguing that the private sphere was in fact a primary site of power relations and of gendered inequality. They emphasized the way in which personal circumstances are structured by public factors. Women's lives are regulated and conditioned, for example, by the legal status of wives, by government policies on childcare, by the allocation of welfare benefits, by labour laws and the sexual division of labour, and by laws on rape, abortion, sexual harassment. ' "Personal" problems can thus be solved only through political means and political action'(Pateman 1997: 117). Women's everyday experience in patriarchal societies has confirmed this intertwining of the public and the private and the impossibility of a real separation between the two spheres. Moreover, feminists have challenged the moral associations of this public–private divide, which suggest that there is an equivalent division between justice – which is a public value – and care – which is a private one. As a result, a moral boundary is erected between public and private (Tronto 1993), and as Ruth Lister (1997: 120) explains: 'The ideological construction of the public–private divide thereby contributes to the opposition of justice and care and to the convenient camouflaging of men's dependence upon women for care and servicing.'

The division between public and private is thus criticized by feminists for its practical and moral implications. And they argue that because of women's particular experience of the interconnection between the two supposedly separate spheres, and because of their revolt against their exclusion from the political sphere, women have thus been well placed to pioneer a theoretical and practical approach to politics which has widened the previously narrow boundaries of the political and thus challenged the boundary between public and private. On a theoretical level, feminists have analysed the ways in which the 'public' sphere of politics influences the private lives of women, and also the ways in which power relations in the so-called private sphere create situations of oppression and domination. On a practical level, feminists point out that women have also challenged traditional definitions of the political by pioneering and becoming highly involved in forms of political action outside of the mainstream institutional politics that men have for so long dominated. Thus, women challenged the boundaries between 'formal' and 'informal' politics. Lister (1997), for example, makes a strong argument for analysing women's participation in terms of local community-based action as well as the more traditional forms of participation which have been so male-dominated.

But how should the public–private divide be seen in feminist theory of politics? Do feminists want to get rid of this division altogether and make all areas of life public? And does the claim that 'the personal is political' mean that feminists sanction state intervention in all areas of a person's private and personal life? In fact, there have been only a few feminists who believed that the division between the public and the private should be abolished altogether, arguing that, as this division has served to sustain male power for so long, the two categories of public and private should be completely dissolved. Others have argued for a reconstruction and rearticulation of the division in order to create boundaries consistent with gender relations of equality and not domination. As Lister explains, this rearticulation of the public–private divide comprises three elements. These are, first, 'the deconstruction of the sexualised values associated with public and private so that it is the gendered quality of the distinction and of the attributes associated with each of the spheres that is dissolved, rather than the distinction itself' (1997: 121); second, a rejection of the rigid ideological separation between public and private in an acknowledgement of the many varied ways in which the two spheres overlap and interact; and third, a recognition that the boundaries between the two domains of public and private are not fixed but are constantly changing and are a site of constant struggle. Any definition of a public–private boundary cannot therefore be fixed and universal but will be constantly evolving to mirror social change and evolution. Rather than attempt any universal redefinition of these boundaries, it may therefore be more productive to undertake specific analyses of the ways in which particular state policies affect women's position in society: 'public–private splits *are* significant, but it is an important task to clarify what these mean in practice' (Dahlerup 1987: 108, original emphasis). One of the areas where this more specific analysis has been focused in recent years is on women's relationship to the welfare state and the way that the public cuts in welfare spending have affected women's lives. We will return to this issue later in the chapter.

Women and political participation: the fight for suffrage

One consequence of the feminist critiques of the public–private divide and of the way that this division, and the very narrow definition of the political that it entailed, has structured political institutions, has been a move away from engagement with these institutions and an investment in other, less formal forms of political action and activism. While women have been engaging in other, alternative forms of political action, however, there has still been a continued pressure from different feminist groups for inclusion and participation in the formal political process, and different feminisms have been divided over the best means to make their demands felt, whether within traditional political channels or outside them. The pressure for inclusion in the political process and for full citizenship for women has existed for centuries, for as the doctrine of 'the rights of man' spread through Europe and the United States in the eighteenth and nineteenth centuries, so women began to claim equal rights for themselves. In 1791, for example, Olympe de Gouges, a French revolutionary, published her *Declaration of the Rights of Woman and Citizen* in response to the revolution's *Declaration of the Rights of Man and Citizen* (1789) which, as we have seen, had excluded women from active political citizenship. In this declaration de Gouges argued that women were naturally men's equals, that they were individuals just as men were, and that they should, therefore, have all the rights that men did. Her famous statement that 'Woman has the right to mount to the scaffold; she ought equally to have the right to mount to the tribune' was taken up as a rallying call for feminists after de Gouges herself had been guillotined. De Gouges was not the first or the only feminist to speak out at this time, and during the nineteenth century pressure began to build in favour of women's rights. Perhaps the best-known example of feminist action against women's exclusion from the political sphere is the suffrage movement, which became prominent in Europe and the United States at the end of the nineteenth and the beginning of the twentieth century. At this time the vote became a symbol for many different feminist movements and campaigns, and it can be argued that support for women's suffrage became in some way a 'litmus test' of feminist credentials (Delmar 1986). The issue of suffrage and the campaigns for the vote for women, however, provide an excellent illustration of the way in which a supposedly 'unifying' issue can act to mask important differences between different feminist viewpoints. There were many feminists for whom the vote was not considered a central issue, and there were also different theoretical positions and justifications in arguing for women's suffrage. For many, the issue of suffrage was one that was not just a question of 'women's rights' but of 'human rights', as large sections of the male population were also denied the vote. It was, therefore, not perceived as a key area of inequality between women and men, and not one that was central to the feminist cause. Mary Wollstonecraft, for example, argued that:

I really think that women ought to have representatives, instead of being arbitrarily governed without having any direct share allowed them in the deliberations of government. But, as the whole system of representation in this country is only a convenient handle for despotism, they need not complain, for they are as well represented as a numerous class of hard working mechanics.

(Wollstonecraft 1995: 166)

For those who believed, on the other hand, that women's suffrage was a key issue, there were divisions concerning their justifications for their claims. These women were again confronted with the paradox of trying to overcome exclusion based on definitions of sexual difference, but at the same time reinforcing this sexual difference through affirmation of a group identity as 'women'. As Scott (1996: x) points out:

The terms of women's exclusion from politics involved attempts to produce an authoritative definition for gender. These terms confronted feminists with an irresolvable dilemma. It has come to us in the form of debates about 'equality' or 'difference'. Are women the same as men? And is this sameness the only basis upon which equality can be claimed? Or are they different and, because or in spite of their difference, entitled to equal treatment? Either position attributes fixed and opposing identities to women and men, implicitly endorsing the premise that there can be an authoritative definition for sexual difference.

This was a paradox that the suffragettes had to face. Women had been excluded from full political citizenship on the basis of presumed 'natural' sexual difference, which meant that men were more rational than women. So, to fight this exclusion women had to claim that they were not in fact different, but were men's equals – equally as rational and capable of taking part in the political sphere. On the other hand, in mobilizing as women and claiming rights for women they were affirming their identity as women, and thus reinforcing the existence of sexual difference. And although some suffragettes were eager to deny sexual difference as far as they could, others sought to emphasize women's specific qualities, which they thought justified their inclusion in the political sphere.

These different arguments remain present in feminist discourse today. For, although women have achieved suffrage (sooner or later) in all Western democracies, they have found that the right to vote does not automatically lead, as the suffragettes might have expected, to full political citizenship. An important element of political citizenship is clearly political participation, and, for most feminists, this participation must be more than a chance to vote every few years, to be valid. One element of political citizenship which has become a thorny issue is that of representation. Despite having the right to eligibility and the right to vote, women are still underrepresented in most parliaments and governments worldwide, and in other elected decision-making bodies, both local and national.

Widening the boundaries of the 'political': towards an informal politics

Partly as a result of this failure of representative institutions to open up to women, many of the 'second-wave' feminists of the 1960s and 1970s expressed their disappointment in the perceived failure of formal political institutions to admit women and to consider women's rights by moving their focus of action away from these institutions. It can be argued that the feminisms of the late 1960s and 1970s onwards enlarged the field of the political so far as to diminish the importance and relevance of parliamentary and government institutions as a focus for women's struggles. As Eliane Viennot (1984: 155) explains with reference to the French feminist movement, the MLF (Mouvement de libération des femmes):

> Whilst feminists at the beginning of the twentieth century situated their action above all in the field of institutional politics: the right to vote, legislation, etc. . . . The MLF of the 1970s, on the contrary, whilst affirming the highly political character of their actions, expressed themselves above all on issues regarding specific oppressions of women (abortion, rape, health, education, culture . . .), refusing any type of intervention (other than critical) at the heart of institutional politics.

This move of their activism away from formal political institutions meant that many feminists were keen to stress women's political action at an informal, associational level. As these feminists pointed out, however, this type of politics has often been rendered invisible by classic, 'masculine' definitions of power as a top-down concept, embodied in formal representative institutions, rather than as a grass-roots, bottom-up activity, which is the type of politics that women have most successfully engaged in.

A theoretical underpinning for this move away from formal

political institutions as a site of feminist struggle was provided by books such as Kate Millett's *Sexual Politics* (1970). Millett begins her work by asking the question 'can the relationship between the sexes be viewed in a political light at all?' Her answer is yes, but only if you define politics in a certain way: 'This essay does not define politics as that relatively narrow and exclusive world of meetings, chairmen, and parties. The term "politics" shall refer to power-structured relationships, arrangements whereby one group of persons is controlled by another' (1970: 5). This recognition that power relations exist everywhere in society – in personal relationships as well as in formal political institutions – was a vital step in the understanding of women's dominated position in society, and, indeed, this is one respect in which feminism has had a major influence on social and political theory. Some would even argue that: 'The most important contribution of feminism to social theory has been the recognition that power relations operate within primary social relations as well as within the more impersonal secondary social relations of the civil and political domains' (Yuval-Davis 1997: 13). This claim that power relations exist everywhere also leads some feminists to argue for the abandonment of the state as a distinct category of feminist analysis. Judith Allen (1990), for example, argues that feminism does not need a theory of the state, as it requires and provides theories of other, more significant categories and processes. In fact, the retention of the state as a category of analysis actually hampers feminist theorizing, in that it obscures other processes of domination and connections that feminists may want to make between them.

There is a danger, however, that in arguing that everything is political, the meaning of politics is diluted so much that it is useless as a distinct category of analysis. As Squires (1999: 23) comments:

> The idea that politics is power, coupled with the adoption of an extensive heterogeneous conception of power, encouraged many feminist theorists to consider politics as largely indistinguishable from anything else. This has generated a huge series of reflections on 'the politics of ...' (sexuality, reproduction, identity, housework, fashion ...) but does little to define the nature of the political itself.

In an attempt to redress this balance there have been a number of recent feminist works on politics, citizenship and the state (for example, Lovenduski and Norris 1996; Lister 1997; Phillips 1998). These all stress, in different ways, the importance of politics as a distinct category of analysis for feminists. They also argue for the need to retain the state as a separate and distinct area of study, as the state and formal political institutions remain the sites to which the exercise of individual and collective rights are tied (Yuval-Davis and Anthias 1989).

The feminist disengagement from formal political institutions and processes in the 1960s and 1970s was not unanimous and there have always been feminists who have sought to increase women's representation in national and local governments and representative bodies. And in recent years it seems that there has been a reconsideration of the importance of mainstream politics by feminists, and a renewed interest from feminist movements in formal political institutions and women's exclusion from them. Although, as was highlighted above, feminist analyses of the political have often shifted the emphasis away from formal political institutions and on to women's informal political activism at a community-based level, many feminists have also recently recognized that acknowledgement of this different form of political activism is not enough and if they are confined to this informal politics women risk remaining marginalized. Their political activity and status will be 'different' but not 'equal' (Lister 1997). While recognizing that power exists not only in formal political institutions, there is a growing realization among feminists that these institutions remain an important site of struggle and power and that if women wish to really challenge male domination, they must therefore enter the arena of formal politics. As Stacey and Price (1981: 189) conclude:

> If women wish to make changes in the societies they live in, they must seek and achieve power positions. It is essential that women should enter the political arena since the societies are all male dominated, for men certainly cannot be relied upon to initiate or carry through the necessary changes.

Women and representation: campaigns for gender parity

The recognition that women must gain access to formal political institutions as an integral part of their strategy to overcome the male domination of society has led feminists to a renewed interest in the reasons for women's exclusion from political institutions (Freedman 1997). Campaigns have been started to facilitate the entry of more women into these institutions through various means, including financial aid to women candidates (through organizations such as Emily's List, which was founded in the United States and later also operated in Britain), education for girls and young women to encourage them to consider a political career, workshops to help train women as potential candidates, or campaigns for legal reform to enshrine quotas or laws on gender parity in political constitutions.

A sign of this reinvestment in formal political processes and institutions has been the way in which feminists have become active members of political parties and have begun to claim parity of political representation, aiming to work from within the parties to change the political system and increase women's representation (Lovenduski and Norris 1993). In the Scandinavian countries, increasing political mobilization and pressure from women's groups for inclusion in representative institutions was successful in bringing women's issues on to the mainstream party agenda (Sainsbury 1994) and eventually led to the introduction of quota systems to ensure equal representation for women. In other countries, feminist pressure for this type of 'positive discrimination' has been less successful and has often been challenged legally – a law passed in 1982 by the French socialist government to ensure that party lists for elections comprised no more than 75 per cent of candidates of the same sex was judged unconstitutional by the Conseil Constitutionnel (Constitutional Council) on the grounds that it breached the universal basis of citizenship and discriminated between citizens on the basis of sex (Jenson and Sineau 1995). Similarly, the British Labour Party's attempt to introduce all-women shortlists, voted for at its 1993 conference (Short 1996), was challenged in the courts by men, who claimed that this policy was discriminatory on the basis of sex. So, it seems that often attempts to introduce real equality into the political arena have foundered because they were seen to be breaching the formal universal equality on which Western political systems are based, a universalism that feminists argue has in fact excluded women since the outset (Fraisse 1995).

In the past decade, however, a European-originated initiative on gender parity seems to be having positive effects as feminists renew their efforts to gain equal representation for women in political decision-making bodies. This feminist activity in favour of parity has been particularly strong in France, where, under pressure from the Mouvement pour la parité (a federation of diverse feminist organizations campaigning on this issue), a constitutional amendment was passed in January 2000 to enable action to ensure gender parity through means such as withdrawal of financial support for parties who do not present an equal number of male and female candidates in elections. And this movement towards legal guarantees of women's representation is not limited to Western countries. India is also debating legislation on women's equal representation in elected assemblies. This type of legislation can be seen as a victory for feminist campaigns, and many feminists hope that it may help to change the face of institutional politics, although this is a contested point.

In fact, feminists typically use three types of argument in campaigning for quotas for women's representation or for gender parity. They may argue first that equal representation for women is a matter of justice, 'that it is patently and grotesquely unfair for men to monopolize representation' (Phillips 1998: 229). This may seem a clear-cut and unproblematic argument in favour of gender parity, but, as Anne Phillips (1998) indicates, it relies on a strong feminist position on the current sexual division of labour, and also depends on a particular interpretation of the act of political representation. These difficulties mean that the most satisfactory version of this argument from the standpoint of justice may come if the question is turned around and the burden is placed on men to justify their domination of political representation, but, as Phillips (1998: 233) concludes, although this is the most promising form of the argument it is still problematic:

> There is no argument from justice that can defend the current state of affairs; and in this more negative sense, there is an argument from justice for parity between women and men. But there is still a troubling sense in which the argument overlooks what is peculiar to representation as a political act.

The other two types of argument in favour of gender parity are more concerned with the peculiarities of the process of representation and with women's position in this process.

A second argument used in favour of parity democracy is that only women can adequately represent women's interests. This question of the representation of interests is a highly contested one that we will return to in the next section. This second argument is, however, more defined than the third, which relates to the supposedly beneficial influence that the presence of women would have on the functioning of political institutions. This type of argument is often rather less developed than the previous two, and includes a range of different feminist positions. Some of these arguments depend on a (sometimes rather crude) belief in women's moral difference, which would have an impact on political institutions and the content of decision-making. Eliane Viennot (1994: 71), for example, makes a plea in favour of French women's demands for parity in which she argues that the Gulf War would probably have been avoided or at least much moderated if women had been equally represented in parliament at the time. Others imagine that having more women in representative institutions could lead to a challenge to the party system, with more cross-party voting and alliances between women of different parties, or that women could bring their experiences of informal politics into the formal political arena and thus create a more open political culture (Hedlund 1988). Critics of these ideas may point to the fact that women who are already present in political institutions show little sign of developing such open or cross-party politics, but a part of the argument in favour of the idea that women will change politics is that of the 'critical mass', with feminists arguing that the pressures from party, and so on, are so strong that a large number of women will have to be present in representative institutions before these women have the freedom to exercise their different approach to politics. As Phillips (1998) argues, though, this type of justification for parity democracy finally only makes sense if it is placed in the context of a general project for widening participation and enhancing democracy. Perhaps if feminist claims for equal representation lead to a general reassessment of our democratic systems and an opening up of the representation process, then this will be seen as a real achievement for the proponents of parity democracy.

Women's interests: A 'politics of ideas' or a 'politics of presence'

The second argument often used in favour of gender parity is, as mentioned above, that women's presence in representative institutions is necessary to ensure that women's interests are represented in and by those institutions. As Anna Jónasdóttir (1988: 53) forcefully maintains:

> [Women] must be visible politically as women, and be empowered to act in that capacity, because there is the continual possibility (not necessity) that they may have needs and attitudes on vital issues which differ from those of men. This does not imply that women have no needs and

preferences in common with men. Nor does it imply that these differences only reflect biological distinctions, but it does imply, as extensive
facts in contemporary Western societies indicate, that women and men
are beginning to construct themselves as two basic societal corporations. These developments, which have their origins in the second
wave of the women's movement and its ensuing mobilization of women,
can be found more or less within every area of social life.

This claim that women must be present in representative institutions in order to represent women's interests is part of what Anne
Phillips has called a 'politics of presence'. She contrasts this politics
of presence with a 'politics of ideas'. In the model of a politics of
ideas, what is important is the responsiveness of representatives to
their electorate in the policies that they produce; as long as this is
the case, it does not matter who these representatives are, whether
men or women: 'The messages will vary, but it hardly matters if the
messengers are the same' (1995: 6). On the other hand, for a politics of presence, the identity of these 'messengers' is vital – they
must be representative of the electorate in the sense of shared identity and experience, and a vital part of this shared identity and
experience is constituted by gender.

This argument of the necessity for a politics of presence forms one
of the justifications used by feminists for claiming women's equal
representation in the political. This claim was put forcefully, as we
have seen, by Jónasdóttir, but it remains a contested one. The whole
question of the representation of women is, as Virginia Sapiro (1998)
points out, a fairly recent one, as, historically, women were assumed
to be represented in the public sphere by their husbands, and indeed
this was one of the most serious legal objections to women's suffrage.
Since women have been granted suffrage and formal political equality, however, the question of their representation has arisen, and
feminists have asked themselves first whether women have a specific
set of interests to be represented, and whether, if this is the case,
political institutions adequately represent and act to further those
interests. The first part of this question – whether women as a group
have a specific set of interests that need representing – is a highly
complex and disputed one, and the answer to it will vary, depending
on different feminists' definitions of women's group identity and,
indeed, their views on whether such a group identity can be defined
at all. It could be argued that differences between women are such
that no common political interests could be shared by them all,
although for some the mere fact of women's exclusion from full

political citizenship is enough to designate them as having a common interest (Jónasdóttir 1988; Lister 1997).

Commonly, in political systems there is a group of issues that are designated as 'women's issues', issues that are perceived as being of specific relevance to women. These issues are usually those closely associated with the private domestic sphere, such as those involved in bringing up children. The relevance of these 'women's issues' can, however, be interpreted in different ways. In her article 'When are interests interesting?', Sapiro argues that women 'do have a distinct position and a shared set of problems that characterize a special interest' (1998: 165). She locates this shared set of problems principally within the family and more exactly in the gendered division of labour within the family, contending that these divisions of labour in private life can define interest groups in politics in the same way as do divisions of labour and stratification in public life. Women are not, however, always conscious of their different social position and their different interests to be represented, and this means that these interests are unlikely to be represented, as 'political systems are not likely to represent previously unrepresented groups until those groups develop a sense of their own interests and place demands on the system' (1998: 167). This explains why consciousness raising is such an important tactic for feminist organizations. Under these conditions, women do seem to be best placed to represent women's interests, although Sapiro argues that women's presence is a necessary but not sufficient condition for the representation of such interests.

The very premises on which Sapiro's argument is based are criticized, however, in a direct response to her article by Irene Diamond and Nancy Hartsock. Diamond and Hartsock (1998: 193) argue that women cannot be treated as an interest group just like any other, because 'if the inclusion of women in politics threatens the most basic structures of society, one cannot fit their concerns into the framework of interests'. They argue instead for a more thorough analysis of the division of labour in private life, and in doing so highlight the way in which different male and female activities lead towards different social understandings. This profoundly different female experience then forms a basis to expose the flaws in the traditional male categories of political analysis, and it calls into question the appropriateness of using the concept of interests to understand politics at all. Instead, this should be replaced with categories such as needs which more adequately capture human experiences and emotions. Unlike Sapiro, then, Diamond and Hart-sock do not believe that women can just be included in the current political system but that the system itself must be redefined if women are to be truly represented. But, together with Sapiro, they are convinced that women are best placed to represent and 'act for' women within the confines of the current political system because only women have the ability to identify issues and problems that affect the lives of large numbers of women but that have so far remained invisible on the political agenda.

Despite very different feminist viewpoints on the existence of women's interests and on the suitability of using interests as a category of political analysis, there does seem to be quite a lot of support for the idea that the presence of more women in representative assemblies would help to raise and articulate problems that women encounter in their lives. Phillips does, however, caution against the unqualified adoption of a 'politics of presence', arguing that a politics of ideas is also required in order to try to guarantee the accountability of representatives. She concludes that 'it is in the relationship between ideas and presence that we can best hope to find a fairer system of representation, not in a false opposition between one or the other' (1998: 25).

Feminism and citizenship

This chapter has so far discussed women's relation to the political sphere, and feminist critiques of the public–private divide and of women's exclusion from full political citizenship. Clearly, however, there is more to citizenship than political participation and representation, and feminists have been at the forefront of recent debates over the definition and redefinition of citizenship in contemporary societies. Citizenship is a contested concept, but for many theorists a starting point in discussions over the meaning of citizenship has been T. H Marshall's 1950 definition, which focuses on three groups of rights granted to individuals by the state, these rights being civil, political and social. Civil rights are those 'necessary for individual freedom – liberty of the person, freedom of speech and thought and faith, the right to own property and to conclude valid contracts, and the right to justice' (1950: 10). Political rights are the rights to elect and take part in the bodies invested with political power. And social rights comprise 'the whole range from the right to a modicum of economic welfare and security to the right to share to the full in the social heritage and to live the life of a civilised being according to the standards prevailing in the society' (1950: 11). The institutions most closely connected with these social rights are the education system and the social services. Marshall argued that these rights had been built up over a period of centuries, with first civil, then political and, finally, social rights being granted.

Feminists have criticized Marshall's schema as inaccurate. Walby (1997) indicates that the different rights were granted to different social groups at differential rates, with countries varying 'as to whether White men, White women, men and women of minority ethnic groups, gained citizenship at the same time or not' (1997: 171). And in the case of some groups in some countries, the order of rights that Marshall described was reversed. British women, for example, campaigned for both civil and political rights during the 'first-wave' feminist movements of the late ninteenth and early twentieth century, and many aspects of civil citizenship were not won until after women had achieved political citizenship rights. Perhaps, however, this notion of citizenship needs to be problematized still further, and, rather than merely analysing the ways in which women have been 'slower' than men to accede to full citizenship rights, we need to ask whether women can be 'included' in this model of citizenship at all – a model that is supposedly universal but that is based on a masculine notion of the individual. Ursula Vogel (1988, 1994), for example, points to the historical significance of married women's exclusion from civil rights on the basis that men would have these rights as representatives of the family. Women were thus connected to civil society through a relationship of dependence, which has had a lasting legacy on the composition of women's social rights. Vogel argues (1994: 86), therefore, that it is pointless to try to insert women into the 'ready-made gender neutral spaces of traditional conceptions of citizenship'.

Women and the welfare state

Feminist redefinitions of the notion of citizenship have often focused particularly on social citizenship and on the specific ways in which the rights of social citizenship, which are defined in a supposedly gender-neutral way, have in fact excluded women because of their particular experiences and positions in society. This analysis of social citizenship rights necessarily often revolves around women's relationship to the welfare state, both as 'producers' and as 'clients'.

The issue of women's relationship to the welfare state is a complex one for feminists, necessitating as it does a detailed analysis of women's dual role both in the domestic sphere and in paid work (Showstack Sassoon 1987). Often a dilemma is raised as, on the one hand, feminists argue that women should stop being exploited at home and enter the labour market, and, on the other, they maintain that women's positions as carers should be supported by the state (Walby 1997: 174). Some feminists such as Lister (1997) advocate that these two options taken together are viable strategies for women to gain equal social citizenship. Others see the two options as perhaps incompatible, highlighting once again the equality–difference debate in feminism. Jane Lewis (1986: 86) indicates the way in which the equality–difference question has structured feminist debates over women's relation to the welfare state, arguing that:

> Feminism has also experienced what is in fact an historical tension between an organisation and practice that starts from women's claims as mothers and one that believed the main task to be the problem of defining and obtaining equality for women as individuals in the public sphere.

A continuing tension exists for women between their roles as wage earners and their roles as unpaid carers – should they seek to claim equal rights to men and abandon their caring roles, or should they demand that these roles be adequately valued?

The development of the welfare state has been one of the major social changes in twentieth-century Europe and the United States, and one that has often been perceived as beneficial to women. Feminists have pointed to the ways in which women were in fact instrumental in bringing about the political reforms that led to the creation of the welfare state, despite their lack of access to the power structures that instituted these reforms (Dale and Foster 1986; Bock and Thane 1991). Although campaigns by women's rights movements for greater social citizenship rights for women had differing degrees of success, Bock and Thane (1991: 15) argue that contemporary welfare states would look very different if it were not for their influence: 'By working with and within other political and intellectual currents of the time as well as by insisting upon their own and unique contributions to society at large, they ensured that women's needs were incorporated into policymaking.' The development of welfare states was thus influenced by women's campaigns and interventions in the policy-making process, and as a result welfare states have undoubtedly conferred material benefits on women. There remains, however, an ambivalence in women's relationship to the welfare state, a tension between demands on them as unpaid carers and expectations that they fulfil a role in paid employment.

As Anette Borchorst and Birte Siim (1987) argue in relation to the position of Denmark and Sweden, one of the main characteristics of the development of the welfare state has been the emergence of a partnership between women and the state. However, this partnership is based on an institutionalization of women's double role as mothers and carers on the one hand, and wage earners on the other. This developing partnership between women and the state can be seen as a move away from women's dependence on men in the private sphere to a dependence on the state in the public sphere. This is especially clear in relation to the well-developed welfare states in Scandinavia. Helga Hernes (1987) analyses Scandinavian welfare states and argues that the transition from private to public forms of dependence accentuates inequalities in terms of power which have existed in the family based on men's provider status, and has moved them to the public sector where they have become a part of organizational hierarchies. In fact, she argues, the incorporation of the new participants into the political process, and the expansion of the tasks of the modern state, has had a particular effect on women, who have become, more than men, dependent on the state both as an employer and as a provider of benefits. At the same time, state hierarchies are still male dominated. So women have moved out of their position of private dependency on men in the home into a position of public dependency on the male-controlled state.

This move from private to public dependency highlighted by Hernes has also been remarked on by other feminists. It seems that the feminist battles for women's citizenship which started with the calls for suffrage and for women's political participation have ended the total exclusion of women from the political sphere. But this move out of the private sphere of the home and into the public arena has not meant a total emancipation for women, who are still underrepresented in positions of power and decision-making and who are often now dependent on the state. For many feminists, the task is now to combat this 'public patriarchy' to which women are subject.

3

Employment and the Global Economy

Feminism has always been concerned in some way with women's participation or non-participation in paid employment. Sheila Rowbotham (1992) describes the activism of women in nineteenth-century radical and socialist movements, women who campaigned not principally for suffrage but rather for women's right to work and to be treated fairly and paid equally to men. Already at this time, women's low wages and poor work conditions were seen as the result of male domination by Frances and James Morrison, the editors of an Owenite trade union paper, *The Pioneer*, who argued that: 'the low wages of woman [sic] are not so much the voluntary price she sets upon her labour as the price which is fixed by the tyrannical influence of male supremacy' (in Rowbotham 1992: 42). In France, too, women activists were calling for measures to re-organize both households and industry to liberate women. An issue of particular concern was that of home work – as employers sought to cut costs by contracting out work to individual home workers, some of the hardest hit were women, who worked enormously long hours for a pittance. But women's demands for reform went further than this, as Rowbotham (1992: 61) explains:

Women workers did not simply say homework should be banned. It was a vital means by which women with children could support themselves. Instead, they proposed that homework be paid the same rate as work in the workshops. They also demanded state child-care, laundries, and restaurants, along with training for women workers. They began to form their own cooperative associations to secure employment, improve conditions, and enable them to run their work places democratically. These cooperative associations extended beyond the workplace. They provided housing and welfare services and they imagined communal housing with gardens and schools and health services for workers on a large scale.

It is clear from these examples that the issues of paid employment, equal salaries and the provision of conditions such as childcare to enable women to work, have been long-term feminist concerns. These concerns with the fairer organization of work have often drawn feminists close to socialist movements, but at the same time there has often been a disappointment with socialism for its failure to address women's oppression in anything other than a marginal fashion. This has been true for many forms of socialism, including Marxism. Marx himself was theoretically committed to the legal emancipation of women and to women's right to work (as opposed to some socialists such as Proudhon, who opposed women's work outside of the home), but for him, as for many other socialists, the struggle for women's liberation was subsumed within the class struggle. This has not stopped feminists from adapting Marxism and using Marxist-based analysis to describe the oppression of women as a class; some of these analyses will be discussed further later in the chapter. It is interesting to note here, however, that even in the early days of women's campaigning for fairer treatment in the workplace, the equality–difference question crept into debates. A fiercely contested issue was that of whether women in the workplace should be treated in exactly the same way as men or whether there should be special protection for women; whether women workers had identical needs to men workers or whether they should separate their cause. An illustration of this dilemma is provided by the German socialist Clara Zetkin, who argued in 1889 that there should be no special protection for women other than that which labour in general demanded against capital, but by 1896 she had changed her position and maintained the need for protective legislation for women (Rowbotham 1992: 146).

As the twentieth century progressed and more and more women entered the labour force, these types of questions about women's work proliferated and feminists continued to debate the ways in which women's engagement in paid employment affected their lives. Although for some feminists this increase in women's employment outside of the home is seen as a positive element in increased equality between men and women, for others it is not such an important factor in reducing gender inequalities, and indeed, some feminists argue that it is an extra burden for women, resulting in a double day's work of paid employment outside of the home and unpaid housework in it. Feminists who have focused on an analysis of women's paid employment have typically sought answers to the questions of why there is a continuing gender segregation in the labour market and why women who do take up paid employment still earn on average less than men. Others have focused on women's unpaid work within the family. Increasing economic globalization has meant, moreover, that these questions can no longer be treated merely in the context of one country, and feminists have thus turned their attention to the international system of production and consumption, and the ways in which the destruction of the natural environment has affected women. We will return to these issues later in the chapter.

Women and paid employment: capitalism and patriarchy

As we pointed out above, two major questions to which feminist analyses of women's participation in paid employment have sought answers are: Why is the labour market segregated in a gendered fashion? And why do women on average still earn less than men? The answers to these two questions are clearly linked: women earn less than men partly or wholly because they are restricted to less valued and less well-paid sectors of the labour market. But how and why has this happened?

Some feminists have sought the answer to these questions through a detailed analysis of what actually goes on in different companies. For example, Rosabeth Moss Kanter (1977) carried out a study of men and women in large corporations in the United States and described the ways in which women are disadvantaged in these corporations. She points to the many ways in which the organizational culture of corporations hinders women's advancement. The management ethic, she argues, is primarily masculine, and corporations also foster male networking which excludes women. This type of analysis will strike a chord with many women employed by such corporations, but it has also been criticized for its focus on small-scale analysis of what goes on in individual corporations rather than attempting a large-scale analysis of gender inequalities within the labour market as a whole and in wider society. Sylvia Walby (1990: 33) argues that Kanter's analysis presumes a structure of gender inequality in wider society, and that:

While she shows how this is played out in the structure of the business corporation, this is not an account of how it is caused. So, while it is a superb analysis in its own terms, it is not a total analysis of the sexual division of labour or of gender relations in general.

Other feminists have examined issues such as sexual harassment in the workplace as an explanation of women's lower status and lower wages in paid employment. Sexual harassment may be seen as part of a continuum of sexual violence including pornography and rape (see Chapter 4 for a further discussion of these issues). Sexual harassment is usually defined as unwanted sexual attentions, and feminists such as Stanko (1988) argue that it is a factor in explaining job segregation, as women in traditionally male sectors of the labour market are more likely to report harassment than women working in traditionally female workplaces. Thus women are more likely to be forced to leave jobs in traditionally male sectors of the economy and conversely are more likely to move to or to be attracted in the first place to traditionally female jobs where the risks of harassment are much less. The importance accorded to sexual harassment as an explanatory factor in analysing job segregation clearly depends on one's view of the centrality of sexuality as an explanation for men's control over and dominance of women. I would argue, however, that, like Kanter's analysis described above, feminists such as Stanko who have documented sexual harassment in the workplace have provided an important but only partial contribution to the explanation of gendered job segregation.

More far-reaching analyses of the sexual division of labour and of women's place in the labour market have been provided by Marxist feminists who have attempted to explain women's place in the labour market through an examination of the capitalist system of production. One variant of this Marxist feminist analysis is the reserve army of labour theory, which comes from Marxist theory of labour. Marx argued that a reserve army of labour was used by capitalism to prevent workers from being able to demand higher wages and better working conditions. When there was a great demand for labour which threatened to push up wages, employers could turn to this reserve to bring in new workers and thus resist any demands from existing workers. Some feminists such as Veronica Beechey (1977) have added a gendered element to this argument and maintained that women in fact constitute a flexible reserve army of labour in this sense. They can be drafted into paid employment when there is demand for labour and when wages are threatening to rise, and then made redundant in conditions of depression when this demand falls and unemployment grows. This is particularly the case for married women, as they are presumed to be financially dependent on their husband's wage and to have another occupation in the home, so they are thus able and willing to move in and out of the workforce as demand dictates. This analysis seems theoretically appealing but it has been criticized as failing to be supported by empirical evidence, which does not show that women necessarily leave the workforce at a greater rate than men in times of economic depression (Walby 1990). Furthermore, this type of analysis may purport to explain why women move in and out of paid employment, but it does not attempt to explain the segregation that exists in the labour market. This lack is symptomatic of a more general problem that has been pointed out in relation to Marxist analyses of women's employment – namely, that in concentrating all explanatory force in the needs of capital, Marxists have overlooked other sources of oppression and discrimination which are either linked to capitalism or totally independent of it. Feminists critical of this prioritization of capitalism as an explanation for women's position in the labour force have pointed to the fact that gendered divisions of labour existed in pre-capitalist societies and thus there must be explanations other than those supplied by capitalism for this division of labour. Some Marxist feminist writers have tried to go beyond this purely economistic explanation of women's oppression and to look at the way in which ideology creates gender divisions. Michèle Barrett (1980), for example, stresses the way in which ideology has a pivotal role in the construction of gender, particularly through the institution of the family and the ideology of familialism. This move away from a purely economic explanation of women's oppression in terms of capital and class meant that some Marxist feminists moved beyond the limits of conventional Marxist feminism in the direction of another type of feminist analysis which analyses women's oppression in terms of both capitalism and patriarchy – namely, 'dual-systems' theory. Such dual-systems analysis can be found in the work of Juliet Mitchell (1971), Heidi Hartmann (1979, 1981) and Sylvia Walby (1990, 1997), among others. Whereas Mitchell combines a nonmaterialist account of patriarchy (centred around psychoanalytic theory) with a materialist account of capitalism, other dual-systems theorists such as Hartmann have provided materialist accounts of both patriarchy and capitalism.

The dual-systems analyses of women's participation in the labour market aim to combine a Marxist class-based analysis of capitalist production with a radical feminist account of gender relations under patriarchy. They attempt to describe how the two systems of capitalism and patriarchy are linked and to analyse the ways in which these two systems lead to women and men performing different economic roles in society. Hartmann, for example, argues that capitalism and patriarchy are linked, but that patriarchy precedes capitalism and is not unique to capitalist societies. For her, it is the sexual division of labour that is the crucial point in women's subordination, and this division of labour occurs in societies that are not capitalist. So patriarchy and capitalism are independent but linked; they are two distinct systems but they are intertwined and create interdependence and solidarity among men, which allows them to dominate women. This domination has its material foundations in men's control over women's labour. Men exclude women from the better paid work and thus keep them at a disadvantage. This allows men who earn more than women to marry women on terms that are favourable to them and that ensure that their wives will be more likely to stay at home and take care of the children and do most of the housework. Because women are often financially dependent on men, they cannot refuse to do this unpaid work in the home; and in a type of vicious circle, the fact that women do unpaid work in the home acts as a barrier to their accessing training and better employment. In addition, men control women's sexuality and reproductive capacities and thus determine when they will have children and in what conditions, which again limits women's access to well-paid jobs.

Critics have argued that this dual-systems theory creates a separation between two spheres – that of the home, which is governed by patriarchy; and that of the world outside the home, which is governed by capitalism. This division, it is argued, is reminiscent of the way in which traditional political philosophy makes the division between the public and the private sphere, and it is not helpful to any progressive analysis. On the other hand, dual-systems theory does have the advantage that it acknowledges that there is not just one overarching explanation for women's oppression. Walby (1990) attempts to develop Hartmann's work further by exploring tensions between capitalism and patriarchy and focusing more on the way in which racism interacts with both these systems. Walby also stresses the importance of the effects of international relations on gendered relations in employment. Although some socialist feminists such as Alison Jaggar (1983) argue against dual-systems theory and try to search for an overarching explanation for women's oppression – Jaggar does this through the use of the concept of 'alienation', which she maintains is a concept that can capture the insights of Marxism while moving beyond a narrow class-based analysis and incorporating other explanatory elements such as psychoanalysis, radical feminist notions of sexuality, and so on – I would argue that any theory which attempts to explain women's oppression through one overarching concept risks diminishing the importance of differences among women in the search for theoretical unity. Dual-systems theory moves in the direction of widening rather than narrowing the search for the basis of women's oppression. When the diversity of women's experiences of the gendered labour market and the sexual division of labour throughout the world is considered, it seems vital that feminists move in the direction of widening the search for the explanation of men's control of women's labour, and that they take account of the many forms that this control may and has taken over time and in different places.

Women as unpaid carers: the wages for housework debate

So far, we have considered some feminist approaches to women's paid employment and to the segregation of the labour market. Another closely linked issue, and one that has concerned feminists, is that of women's unpaid labour in the home. As outlined above, this unpaid labour is seen by many feminists as the product of patriarchal and capitalist systems of production which give men power over women through a sexual division of labour. The problem of unpaid domestic work is, however, a thorny one which again pushes feminists into an equality–difference type argument. On the one hand, some feminists have argued that women should abandon domestic work and attempt to seek equality in engaging in paid employment just as much as men do. On the other hand some feminists have argued that the unpaid work that women do in the home and as carers is just as valuable as paid employment, and it should be recognized and valued as such.

One approach to the dilemma of how to treat women's work in the home has been to demand wages for housework. This idea was developed by Mariarosa Dalla Costa and Selma James in a 1972 book entitled *The Power of Women and the Subversion of the Community*. Dalla Costa and James adapted Marx's theory of value arguing that women's unpaid work in the home was vital for capitalism as it produced surplus value. Women, they maintain, are exploited by the capitalist system as unpaid workers, undertaking all the domestic work, childrearing and caring which are necessary for the continuation of the capitalist system. The household where this unpaid labour takes place is thus the central site of women's struggle for emancipation. Women must fight for recognition of the value of the work that they do at home, and demand that they should be paid for this work. Dalla Costa and James argue that it is the state and not individual men who should pay these wages for housework, as it is the state that is one of the major beneficiaries of capitalism. If women do not receive adequate recognition and recompense for their housework, then they should strike. Some women have already undertaken some form of strike action: a woman who divorces her husband, for example, is refusing the work that accompanies the status of wife. Or a woman who chooses to have an abortion is refusing the work involved in bearing and bringing up a child. These acts of refusal are, in this view, part of a potentially powerful revolt by women against the capitalist system which oppresses them.

This argument for waged housework has been strongly criticized by other Marxist feminists who find Dalla Costa and James' arguments theoretically untenable, and by other feminists who find the idea of waged housework ideologically undesirable. Although it is undeniably true that women still do most of the unpaid housework and caring in our society and that they receive little or no recognition for this work, is instituting a system of state-paid wages for housework the right solution to the problem? Although intuitively one might think that it is highly desirable that women are rewarded for their unpaid labours, it can be argued that a system of wages for housework would merely institutionalize and formalize a divide which is already existent, and act to reinforce the division of labour between men and women, rather than questioning this division itself.

Christine Delphy (1984) also analyses women's exploitation as unpaid workers in the home, but, unlike Dalla Costa and James, she argues that the main beneficiary of this unpaid work is not the capitalist state but individual men. Household or domestic production, Delphy maintains, is a distinct mode of production governed by patriarchy, a mode of production in which there are two classes: women/housewives who are the producers and men/husbands who exploit them and profit from their labour. If, as Delphy argues, it is men who profit directly from women's unpaid work in the home, and not the capitalist state, then feminists must struggle to try to change the relationships between men and women under patriarchy which make this exploitation possible. As Walby (1990: 89) points out, feminist struggles (among other factors) have led to significant changes in the household and the relationships between men and women in the family:

> Women are no longer necessarily bound to an individual husband who expropriates their labour till death does them part. Instead, increasing numbers of women change husbands, have children without husbands and engage in work for an employer other than their husband. Women spend a smaller proportion of their life-time's labour under patriarchal relations of production, although while they are full-time housewives they spend as many hours on this labour as did women many decades earlier. Women from different ethnic groups vary as to the extent to which they are engaged in these patriarchal production relations.

Many of these changes have obviously benefited women, but they have not abolished the unequal relationships between men and women in the family sphere. Women still do most of the unpaid work of carers in society even if this is not always within the framework of the traditional nuclear family. In fact, the changes in the structure of domestic or household production can be seen as part of the move from a private to a public form of dependency, as discussed in the last chapter. Following from this it can be argued that feminists must tackle the problems of economic and of social policy as inextricably linked – it is no use if women achieve equal pay in the labour market if at the same time they are still carrying out the role of unpaid carers at home; similarly, merely rewarding women's caring work in the home (usually through the provision of state benefits) will not be sufficient if inequalities persist in paid employment. Yet again we see the need underlined by feminists to rethink the boundaries between the public and the private and to reassess women's work across these boundaries.

The international economy: women as producers and consumers

Earlier in this chapter we pointed to the need to analyse women's role in paid and unpaid employment, not only in one country but in

an international context. This becomes more and more necessary as
the world's economy becomes increasingly globalized, with an
increasing number of large multinational companies structuring
manufacturing and consumption. As Patricia Williams (1993: 118)
maintains, we have to think about the realities of a world where
national boundaries figure less in people's fortunes than the con-
figurations of multinational corporations:

> Local disputes about discrimination in the workplace cannot be
> conceived of as simply local any more: labor problems and civil rights
> violations are not just matters of our laws – not in a world of free trade
> zones, of manufacturing islands whose operations can shift almost
> overnight from North Carolina to Mexico, or to Thailand, Los
> Angeles, or the Philippines.

This global economy, feminists argue, oppresses women in specific
ways both as producers and as consumers. This oppression occurs
in the context of the colonial and postcolonial world order which
presses Western, 'Eurocentric' models of development on to the
Third World. Maria Mies (1986; Mies and Shiva 1993) forcefully
attacks what she calls the 'myth of catching-up development' – in
other words, development strategies based on the assumption
(either explicit or implicit) that the model of the good life is that
prevailing in the affluent societies of the United States, Europe and
Japan, and that 'underdeveloped' countries can reach this good life
by following the development path set out for them by these 'developed' ones. 'These affluent countries and classes, the dominant sex
– the men – the dominant urban centres and lifestyles are then perceived as the realized utopia of liberalism, a utopia still to be
attained by those who apparently still lag behind' (Mies and Shiva
1993: 55). In fact, this ideology is essential to uphold and legitimize
the constant growth and accumulation model of modern industrial
society, and it results not only in impoverishment for the people of
the Third World, but in ecological destruction, and in the continuing oppression of women as this model of development has clearly
gender-differentiated consequences.

This concern with the way in which Eurocentric trade and
development policies have gender-differentiated consequences is
shared by other feminists (Peterson and Runyan 1993) who have
attempted to examine the origins of such policies in the colonial
period when a Western division of labour was imposed on many
African and Asian cultures. In many cases, this resulted in women

becoming more marginalized in the production process as the colonizers forced the colonized to grow cash crops. As the cash crop became the main crop, so new economic arrangements between men and women and new attitudes of male social and economic superiority developed (Ogundipe-Leslie 1993: 108). Today this colonial exploitation continues in more advanced forms with what Mies (Mies and Shiva 1993: 58) describes as the 'externalization of costs' from the industrialized countries to the Third World. No longer is it merely raw materials which are exported to industrialized countries from their colonies; now those former colonies are increasingly the sites of production itself because their workers can be paid far less than workers in the industrialized countries. Women are the optimal labour force in the Third World since they can be paid even less than men. At the same time, women in the industrialized world are exploited through what Mies calls 'housewifization', a historical process necessary for the growth of industry through which women were and are mobilized as the primary consumers of the products of this industry. Mies argues that:

> These two processes of colonization and housewifization are closely and causally interlinked. Without the ongoing exploitation of external colonies – formerly as direct colonies, today within the new international division of labour – the establishment of the 'internal colony', that is, a nuclear family and a woman maintained by a male 'breadwinner' would not have been possible.
>
> (Mies 1986: 110)

Mies' analysis, although open to theoretical and empirical criticism, is provocative in illustrating the interconnectedness between the oppression of women in Third World countries and that of women in industrialized countries. The exploitative structures of capitalism and colonialism, she argues, have also removed much of the basis for international female solidarity because women's interests in different parts of the world, as defined by these systems, have become antagonistic. For example, it may be in the interests of women working in the clothing industry in the Third World to receive higher wages, but this would mean that clothes would cost more to women in industrialized countries, which would be against their interests as consumers. The solution, as Mies sees it, is an end to the 'catch-up' model of development and moves to liberate the consumer, a liberation which would, she argues, benefit women worldwide. Mies' claims over the 'housewifization' of women in the

industrialized countries may have to be qualified because, as we
have already pointed out, more and more women in the industrialized countries are actually entering the labour market (albeit often
in poorly paid, part-time or temporary jobs). In this case, can these
women really be defined first and foremost as housewives who must
consume the products made by exploited Third World women.
What Mies has highlighted, however, is the interlinked nature of
the way in which men dominate and control women in the global
economy. As is the case with women in industrialized countries,
women in the Third World are in many cases doing a double day's
work – employed in production outside the home and then bur-
dened with much of the domestic work in the household (Brydon
and Chant 1989). As Mohanty (1988) points out, however, the
sexual division of labour can mean different things for different
women across the world, and these differences must be considered
by feminists fighting to end this sexual division of labour and to
ensure that women are not exploited in either paid or unpaid
employment.

Feminism and the environment

One of the consequences of the growth of the world economy and
the promotion of Eurocentric models of development has been the
increasingly rapid destruction of the world's ecosystem. Some
feminists like Vandana Shiva have argued that ecology is a specific
feminist issue and have developed what can be called an 'ecofeminism'. Shiva (1988) proposes an ecofeminism which argues that
before the rise of Western colonialism and Western science,
indigenous peoples throughout the world had close and relatively
harmonious relations with the natural world. Natural forces were
typically seen as feminine because they represented the generative
powers of fertility and birth. A 'feminine principle' existed, a reflection of women's particular relationship to nature through the reproductive and productive work of giving birth to children and feeding
them and keeping them healthy as they grow. This feminine principle ensured that the natural environment was not abused but was
cared for and used carefully. This relationship to nature and to natural resources was seriously damaged by the rise of Western
colonialism, which undermined communal land use and women's
land rights, as we have seen, and by Western science, which transformed the global view of nature, seeing it as merely a resource for

men's benefit and not something to be revered and respected as it had been. Thus the feminine principle was inversed, with nature still seen as feminine, but now a passive resource instead of a powerful resource. This reversal paved the way for ecological destruction, overuse of land and the spread of harmful technology. The only way to escape from the continuous cycle of ecological crises would be to revert to women's earlier relationship to the environment and to promote a 'return to nature'. Women's knowledge, Shiva maintains, is vital to the maintenance of biodiversity. It is different knowledge from that of men; a knowledge that makes connections between the different sectors of agricultural production, but one that has often remained invisible.

> The invisibility of women's work and knowledge arises from the gender bias which has a blind spot for realistic assessment of women's contributions. It is also rooted in the sectoral, fragmented and reductionist approach to development which treats forests, livestock and crops as independent of each other.
>
> (Mies and Shiva 1993: 167)

If the world's ecosystem and biodiversity are to be conserved, it is therefore vital to start listening to women and taking their knowledge seriously.

Ecofeminism has been criticized for reproducing an essential division between men and women, culture and nature, in its argument that women are closer to nature and have greater knowledge of biodiversity and so on. To this charge, ecofeminists have argued back, saying that they are not positing an essential, fixed and universal difference between men and women but are merely trying to reclaim the value of terms that have been devalued by patriarchal Western dichotomies that associate men with culture and reason, and women with nature and emotion. As Mary Mellor (1996: 134) points out:

> There have been many feminist critiques of the Western concept of the 'human' as representing white, bourgeois, male interests, values and experience. The case made by both ecocentrists and ecofeminists is that the Western model of modernity based on this 'human' is achieved at the expense of both women and nature. Western notions of self-determination and autonomy have at their centre the idea of the transcendence of the natural world. Biology (bodies) and the ecosystem (nature) are external to the social.

A further critique that may be levelled against ecofeminism is that ecology is not a central concern for the poor women in the Third World who are desperately trying to find enough food to survive and to feed their children. Ecological concerns in this case may be seen as a luxury of richer women who have the leisure to concern themselves with the problems of the ecosystem. An African feminist, 'Molara Ogundipe-Leslie (1993: 104), argues that 'the problems of ecology and eco-systems are not a priority in Third World countries; neither should they be named before the very serious problems of socioeconomics are mentioned'. This is a valid point, but nevertheless even if one recognizes that ecological concerns must take second place to the socioeconomic problems of the Third World, ecofeminists such as Shiva have made an important contribution in signalling the ways in which women's specific knowledge is often 'invisible' – and this may be true not only of environmental knowledge but of other forms of knowledge as well. This invisibility of women's knowledge and of women themselves is an issue that feminists must address if they wish to transform international economics and international politics. As Cynthia Enloe (1990: 198) argues: 'Women need to be made visible in order to understand how and why international power takes the forms it does.'

4
Sexuality and Power

Sexuality is a contested political issue for feminists, and has been since the nineteenth century (Jackson and Scott 1996) and even before. In 1918, a US feminist, Crystal Eastman, wrote:

> Feminists are not nuns. That should be established. We want love and to be loved, and most of us want children, one or two at least. But we want our love to be joyous and free – not clouded with ignorance and fear. And we want our children to be deliberately, eagerly called into being, when we are at our best, not crowded upon us in times of poverty and weakness. We want this precious sex knowledge not just for ourselves, the conscious feminists; we want it for all the millions of unconscious feminists that swarm the earth, – we want it for women.
>
> (quoted in Rowbotham 1992: 224)

This desire echoes feminists' continuing concern with giving women control over their own bodies, providing them with the power and the knowledge to enjoy their sexuality and to have children if and when they wish. At the same time as Eastman was writing, feminists in Europe were fighting to bring women the right to control their fertility. Often this struggle was in the face of fierce opposition – in France, for example, a 1920 law outlawed not only the use of contraception and abortion, but also the diffusion of any propaganda or information on the subject (Reynolds 1996). Although women have made progress in these areas since then, through developments such as effective and safer contraception and abortion, these are still not available to all women worldwide. Moreover, the development of new reproductive technologies can be seen either as a benefit or as an attempt to take away some of the control that women have gained over their childbearing capacities.

Women's lack of control over their bodies and their sexuality is, for feminists, a part of men's domination of women. And whereas for some feminists sexuality and the issues surrounding it are less central to women's oppression than other economic and political factors, for others sexuality is the very key to men's domination of women. Catharine Mackinnon, for example, argues that sexuality constitutes gender. In other words, there is no separation between the concepts of gender and sexuality; male and female do not exist outside of the eroticization of dominance and subordination. As she maintains:

> Sexuality, then, is a form of power. Gender, as socially constructed embodies it, not the reverse. Women and men are divided by gender, made into the sexes as we know them, by the social requirements of heterosexuality, which institutionalize male sexual dominance and female sexual submission. If this is true, sexuality is the linchpin of gender inequality.
>
> (Mackinnon 1982: 533)

This is a powerful argument, but is one that has been criticized for dismissing the importance of other articulations of male power not primarily through sexuality (Walby 1990). Whether sexuality is viewed as the primary form of oppression of women or as one form of oppression among others, it is, however, agreed by many feminists that women need far greater control over their own bodies and their sexuality. In this chapter we will explore some of the debates in feminism over issues such as heterosexuality, pornography, rape and reproduction.

Heterosexuality and lesbianism

Stemming from the argument (as made by Mackinnon above) that sexuality is central to men's domination of women comes a feminist questioning of heterosexuality. Feminists have questioned the belief that heterosexuality is a naturally occurring practice or a matter of individual choice and have argued that in fact heterosexual relations are part of a socially constructed system of domination. For some feminists, heterosexuality itself is not incompatible with feminism and women's liberation, but there must be considerable transformations in the ways in which heterosexuality is constructed before it becomes acceptable. For others, the ways in which heterosexuality involves men's domination of women implies that the only true liberation for women will come through an abandonment of heterosexuality and an adoption instead of lesbianism. One of the ways in which men control women through heterosexual relations is through a definition of 'normal' female sexuality. Part of this definition, which Anne Koedt (1972) sets out to demolish, is that of the female vaginal orgasm. Koedt argues that the vaginal orgasm is in fact a myth designed to reinforce male power over women. Although women who fail to have vaginal orgasms have been labelled as frigid by men, in fact the vagina is not a highly sensitive area and it is the clitoris that is central to female sexual sensitivity and pleasure. All orgasms are in reality extensions of sensations from the clitoris and not from the vagina. The myth of the vaginal orgasm has been maintained by men, however, because the best stimulant for the penis is the woman's vagina. Men refuse to see women as total, separate human beings and define them instead in terms of how they benefit men's lives. In terms of sexuality this means that women are not seen as individuals who want to and should share equally in the sex act; they are not seen as people with their own desires. The sexual desires of men are all that is considered important. Furthermore, men fear that they will become sexually expendable if the clitoris is substituted for the vagina as the centre of women's sexual pleasure, and that the institution of heterosexuality itself will be threatened. Koedt argues that women must redefine their sexuality, discarding the idea of sex which has been defined as the norm by men and creating new ways of discovering mutual sexual enjoyment.

Although some feminists believe that sexual relations between men and women can be redefined to result in mutual sexual enjoyment, for others heterosexuality can never be compatible with women's liberty and true sexual pleasure. This latter group of feminists has argued that one cannot be a true feminist without being a lesbian, as 'the very essence, definition and nature of heterosexuality is men first' (Bunch 1986: 131). Lesbianism, in some definitions, may not always involve sexual relationships with women, but just the withdrawal from sexual relationships with men. For example, the Leeds Revolutionary Feminist Group stated that it believed that all feminists could and should be 'political lesbians', by which they meant 'a woman-identified woman who does not fuck men. It does not mean compulsory sexual activity with women' (Onlywomen 1981: 5). The women of the Leeds group argued that the heterosexual couple was the basis of male supremacy and that any woman who slept with a man was collaborating with the enemy. Sexual choice is thus identified as a political act, a decision whether to collaborate in the continuation of male domination or to adopt a stand against it. Sexual preference is not seen as in any way 'natural'. The view that lesbianism is a political choice against male domination and that it does not necessarily involve sexual relations with a woman but merely withdrawal from heterosexuality has, however, been criticized for taking away the positive aspect of the sexual choice to be a lesbian and replacing it with a negative political one. Feminists have thus been drawn into a debate about how lesbianism should be defined – narrowly as a sexual relationship between two women, or more widely.

Adrienne Rich (1980, 1986) is one of those to argue against a narrow, primarily sexual definition of lesbianism, and instead she talks about a 'lesbian continuum'. Within this continuum she includes not only sexual acts but a whole range of 'woman-identified' experience:

> I mean the term *lesbian continuum* to include a range – through each woman's life and throughout history – of woman-identified experience; not simply the fact that a woman has had or consciously desired genital sexual experience with another woman. If we expand it to embrace many more forms of primary intensity between and among women, including the sharing of a rich inner life, the bonding against male tyranny, the giving and receiving of practical and political support . . . we begin to grasp breadths of female history and psychology which have lain out of reach as a consequence of limited, mostly clinical, definitions of 'lesbianism'.
>
> (Rich 1980: 648, original emphasis)

Women can and do move in and out of this lesbian continuum whether they identify themselves as lesbian or not, so this concept of continuum, Rich argues, avoids restrictive definitions of lesbianism and reveals vital continuities between different types of shared female experience. Although this may seem an appealing way out of the difficulties of the definition of what constitutes lesbian experience, and a tempting strategy for unity among women, whatever their sexual identification, it has been criticized by lesbians for taking away the specificity of their sexual experience. Rich's continuum can be seen in this light as a theory that hides differences which some women wish to articulate. In pointing to the wide nature of lesbian experience, however, this idea of a continuum might serve to make lesbianism more visible and thus help to open up to women the full range of sexual choices.

A further debate concerning lesbianism has taken place over the practice of lesbian sado-masochism. This debate, which is closely linked to that over pornography, pits those who believe that lesbian sexuality should eschew the relations of power and domination present in heterosexual sexuality against those who argue that lesbians should be able to engage in the whole range of sexual practices, even if these include dominating and inflicting pain on a partner. Those who argue against lesbian sado-masochism, such as Sheila Jeffreys (1990), claim that this type of sexual activity derives from the domination and control present in masculine sexuality. This type of celebration of power and violence is, she suggests, the opposite of what feminists should seek in a redefinition of female sexuality. In answer to this, those in favour of lesbian sado-masochism and other such practices have argued that these acts have a different meaning when practised between two women, and that the full range of sexual experience should be open to women, whatever this involves. Pat Califia (1981), a member of the group Samois which promotes lesbian sado-masochism, argues strongly against what she sees as the desexualization of lesbianism in a lot of feminist discourse and maintains that any attempt to censor lesbian sado-masochistic porn amounts to repression of many lesbians' sexual fantasies. Feminists, it seems, are agreed that female sexuality must be redefined in order for women to gain true sexual pleasure, but the question is, what should this redefinition of sexuality lead to? Should any sexual act that involves the type of power relations present in current heterosexual practice be avoided? Or can women turn this type of power and domination into positive and pleasurable sexual activities for them?

Pornography

The same questions arise in relation to feminists' views on pornography. Is pornography a central element of men's control over women that is damaging to women's interests? Or can pornography in the right circumstances be used by women as part of a sexual liberation? Should the making and distribution of pornography be limited? Or would this limitation restrict the free expression not just of men but of women themselves? These are key questions in the feminist debate over pornography.

For feminists such as Mackinnon who see sexuality as central to men's control over women, pornography is a vital element of this male domination. Pornography is seen as a central element in men's control over women and is closely linked to sexual violence and rape. As Robin Morgan (1980: 139) argued: 'Pornography is the theory and rape is the practice.' Feminists have argued against pornography on three counts: first that it encourages sexual violence and rape against women, second that in its humiliation of women it is itself a form of sexual violence, and third that women are hurt and economically and sexually exploited in the production of pornography.

Susan Griffin (1981) in her analysis of pornography makes a link between the Western Christian tradition and what she terms the 'pornographic imagination'. Both traditions, she argues, share a contempt for and a fear of women's bodies. Pornography stems from fear because women's bodies arouse desire in men, so men decide that these bodies must be humiliated. Andrea Dworkin (1981) agrees with Griffin that pornography is about male power, arguing that: 'The major theme of pornography as a genre is male power, its nature, its magnitude, its use, its meaning.' She goes on to state that:

> Male sexual domination is a material system with an ideology and a metaphysics. The sexual colonization of women's bodies is a material reality; men control the sexual and reproductive uses of women's bodies. The institutions of control include law, marriage, prostitution, pornography, health care, the economy, organized religion, and systematized physical aggression against women (for instance, in rape and battery).
>
> (Dworkin 1981: 48)

A whole ideology supports this material reality of male domination of women; an ideology based on the notion that men are superior to women because they have a penis, and that it is men's natural right to have physical possession of women and to use women's bodies for sexual or for reproductive purposes. This metaphysical presumption that all women are whores and are there for men's use means that rape or prostitution are not, and cannot be, seen as wrong. Dworkin criticizes those on the Left who call for freedom of expression because this freedom, she argues, merely promotes pornography and thus restricts women's freedom.

Dworkin also points to the racist nature of pornography. This is an issue that has been highlighted by black feminists such as Patricia Hill Collins, who argues that an understanding of racism is essential to any analysis of pornography and sexual violence. She points to the experience of African-American women who were sexually objectified by their white slave masters during the time of slavery, and suggests that: 'African-American women were not included in pornography as an afterthought but instead form a key pillar on which contemporary pornography itself rests' (1990: 50). An examination of the way in which pornography has been central to the oppression of African-American women in terms of race, class and gender can thus offer new routes towards an understanding of power as domination. This understanding of pornography as not only a sexualized but also a racialized manifestation of power is clearly important in any feminist analysis.

The feminist struggle against pornography is not, however, uncontroversial, and it has resulted in serious disagreements between different feminist groups. These have come particularly in the wake of Dworkin and Mackinnon's involvement in helping some American states to draft anti-pornography legislation. This legislation is based on Mackinnon's (1987: 167) definition of pornography as:

> The graphic sexually explicit subordination of women through pictures or words that also includes women dehumanized as sexual objects, things, or commodities; enjoying pain or humiliation or rape; being tied up, cut up, mutilated, bruised, or physically hurt; in postures of sexual submission or servility or display; reduced to body parts, penetrated by objects or animals, or presented in scenarios of degradation, injury, torture; shown as filthy or inferior; bleeding, bruised, or hurt in a context that makes these conditions sexual.

The aim of the laws is to allow individuals to bring legal charges against those producing and displaying pornography for the harm that it has caused. The legislation has, however, been attacked by other feminists, who argue both that it is legally unworkable and, more fundamentally, that it will restrict women's sexual expression as well as men's. As Martha Minow (1990: 157) explains:

> For those who prized the element of the women's movement that advocated sexual liberation for women, the pornography ordinance seemed a new guise for the repression of women's sexual expression. For those who sought room for the creation of sexuality defined by women, whether heterosexual or lesbian, the pornography ordinance seemed a tool of oppression.

Feminists arguing against the anti-pornography legislation feared that Dworkin and Mackinnon were forming a dangerous alliance with the New Right and that their legislation would in fact lead to the censorship of all sexually explicit material, even that produced by and for women. Moreover, it can be argued that arguments such as Dworkin's lead to a binary division being set up between men and women's sexuality and desire, and, as Paula Webster (1981: 49) argues: 'The implications of this neat dichotomization and sex-typing of desire reflect, unchanged, the Victorian ideology of innate differences in the nature of male and female libido and fantasy.' This is a serious criticism of both Griffin and Dworkin's analyses of pornography. In their contention that male sexual violence is the ultimate expression of masculinity, they imply that female sexuality is of a totally different, non-violent and non-dominating nature. Thus, 'the polarization of male and female behavior, and indeed, of male and female "natures" so much deplored in the early writing of the second wave, here reappeared as allegedly fundamental to sexual appetite' (H. Eisenstein 1984: 123). As with other debates on sexuality, feminist analyses of pornography have shown the need to redefine and transform both male and female sexuality; the difficulty is to do this in a non-essentializing and non-exclusionary manner.

Rape and sexual violence

Linked to feminist analyses of pornography as a form of sexual control over women is that of the use of rape and sexual violence as tools of domination. Feminists have seen sexual violence as a continuum running from sexual harassment through to rape and murder. A classic feminist work on rape is Susan Brownmiller's book, *Against Our Will: Men, Women and Rape* (1975). Brownmiller argues that it is sexual violence, and specifically rape and the threat of rape, which gives men control over women. She maintains that all women suffer from this, even if they are not the victims of actual rape – because they are all victims of the threat of rape. It is this fear generated by the threat of rape that keeps women subordinated. Conversely, all men benefit from the fact of rape, even if they are not perpetrators of rape themselves – because the system of rape keeps all women fearful and subordinated to men. Brownmiller makes a parallel between rapists and the Myrmidons, Achilles' hired henchmen:

The Greek warrior Achilles used a swarm of men descended from ants, the Myrmidons, to do his bidding as hired henchmen in battle. Loyal and unquestioning, the Myrmidons served their master well, functioning in anonymity as effective agents of terror. Police-blotter rapists in a very real sense perform a myrmidon function for all men in our society. Cloaked in myths that obscure their identity, they, too, function as anonymous agents of terror. Although they are the ones who do the dirty work, the actual *attentat*, to other men, their superiors in class and station, the lasting benefits of their simple-minded evil have always accrued.

(1975: 204, original emphasis)

Brownmiller supports her view that rape is not about individual acts of male violence but about a system of male control of women with the argument that since rape is not defined as an abnormal offence in criminal law, it is given general legal and social status. Rape, she maintains, is not about momentary loss of control, but is about male aggression and patriarchy. It is not about biology, but about the construction of masculinity in our societies – as evidenced by popular songs and films that portray men as strong and dominating. This construction of masculinity as linked to strength and aggression is a key factor in rape. Socially constructed male aggression is linked not only to rape but to violent pornography and to militarism. War, like rape, forms part of the male system of control of women. During periods of war the rate of rape increases, and this is not just because men have more opportunity in times of war but because war cultivates male violence and the army glorifies such violence. Brownmiller states that:

Once we accept as basic truth that rape is not a crime of irrational, impulsive, uncontrollable lust, but is a deliberate, hostile, violent act of degradation and possession on the part of a would-be conqueror, designed to intimidate and inspire fear, we must look toward those elements in our culture that promote and propagandize these attitudes, which offer men, and in particular, impressionable, adolescent males, who form the potential raping population, the ideology and psychologic encouragement to commit their acts of aggression without awareness, for the most part, that they have committed a punishable crime, let alone a moral wrong. The myth of the heroic rapist that permeates false notions of masculinity, from the successful seducer to the man who 'takes what he wants when he wants it', is inculcated in young boys from the time they first become aware that being a male means access to certain mysterious rights and privileges, including the right to buy a woman's body. When young men learn that females may

be bought for a price, and the acts of sex command set prices, then how
should they not also conclude that that which may be bought may also
be taken without the civility of a monetary exchange?

(Brownmiller 1975: 324)

Brownmiller has been accused of essentialism in her work,
although she does discuss the way that rape has varied in different
social and historical contexts. Perhaps a more pertinent charge
against her has been the accusation that she is insensitive to race in
her analysis of rape – especially in relation to the history of the
United States, where rape was often used as a tool for domination
of white men over their black slaves (see Chapter 5) and where
black men were often falsely accused of raping white women.
Angela Davis (1981) argues that the use of these trumped-up rape
charges against black men in the period immediately following the
end of slavery in the United States was a tactic used to prevent
alliances between white women fighting against sexism and black
men and women fighting against racism. In focusing on sexual violence as the main form of male control of women, Brownmiller
does neglect other forms of domination and control, such as racism.
Her work remains, however, a provocative analysis, and the links
she establishes between rape and other forms of male violence, particularly militarism, have been supported by other feminists such
as Enloe (1983), who describes the effects of militarization on
women's lives. Brownmiller's work, together with that of other
feminists, brought rape on to the feminist agenda and asked the
question of how rape was used to oppress women. As Hester Eisenstein (1984: 34) argues:

> That the question was asked, that it was raised for discussion in the
> first place, was the achievement of the women's movement. In par-
> ticular, it was due to those writers and organizers who first spoke of
> rape as an issue for the consideration of social theory, rather than of
> criminology, and of the ideology of rape as a phenomenon that needed
> explanation, rather than as a natural fact of social life.

Reproduction and mothering

The function of reproduction and the role of motherhood are, for
feminists, one of the highly contested sites. For some, reproduction
and mothering are a burden on women, part of the oppression
which must be lifted; these feminists often see new technologies
that will take the burden of reproduction away from women as the

key to women's liberation. For others, however, motherhood is one
of the great pleasures of being a woman; it is only necessary to
rescue this experience from male control to turn it into a highly
positive one for women. This second group is more wary of new
scientific advances and technologies, which they view as an attempt
by male scientists to maintain and reinforce their control of
women's reproductive capabilities.

Among the first group of feminists perhaps the most well known
is Shulamith Firestone, who argues that the biological division that
gives women the function of reproduction is the cause of women's
oppression. Because she sees reproduction at the very root of men's
domination of women, Firestone maintains that the only way to
truly liberate women is to free them from the burden of reproduction through new scientific technologies. Firestone's book *The
Dialectic of Sex* (1979) places women's liberation at the very heart
of communist revolution. Her 'cybernetic communism' will be
achieved only by the abolition of 'sex class', which in her view goes
deeper than the economic class of traditional Marxist analysis. For
her, the motor of history is not economic but biological, and she
rewrites Engel's definition of historical materialism accordingly:

> Historical materialism is that view of the course of history which seeks
> the ultimate cause and the great moving power of all historical events
> in the dialectic of sex: the division of society into two distinct biological
> classes for procreative reproduction, and the struggle of these classes
> with one another; in the changes in the modes of marriage, reproduc
> tion and child care created by these struggles; in the connected
> development of other physically-differentiated classes (castes); and in
> the first division of labour based on sex which developed into the
> (economic-cultural) class system.
>
> (Firestone 1979: 12)

Women's oppression is thus the primary oppression, 'an oppression
that goes back beyond history to the animal kingdom itself' (Firestone 1979: 12), and this oppression is based on biological oppression. The effects of biology are all-pervading, and women's inferior
social position can be explained by their biology – their reproductive capacity and their weakened physical condition – these biological factors being reinforced by men's development of social
structures that keep women tied to their reproductive role.
Women's liberation is therefore 'a struggle to break free from
oppressive power structures set up by nature and reinforced by
man' (1979: 23). Women must be liberated through the destruction

of this biological oppression, and Firestone believes that this can happen through the development of reproductive technologies that will free women from their biological reproductive capacities. Freeing women from reproduction would also lead, Firestone maintains, to the dissolution of the family unit, with children being brought up by 'households' made up of about 10 adults, and set up to bring up children over a limited period of time. Children would develop no special bonds with their 'parents', but would instead form love ties with people of their own choosing, whatever their age and sex. These new social relations would lead to sexual freedom, and 'adults might return within a few generations to a more natural polymorphous sexuality, the concentration on genital sex and orgasmic pleasure giving way to total physical/emotional relationships that included that' (Firestone 1979: 223).

Firestone's vision may seem far-fetched, the stuff of science-fiction novels or films, but the issues she raises go to the heart of the problem of sexual difference and ways that it might be overcome. As Rosalind Delmar comments in her introduction to *The Dialectic of Sex*:

> The puzzle of sexual difference, refracted through the lens of sexual antagonism, ends with the wish to obliterate that difference entirely. Yet the very forcefulness of the argument demands a rethinking of the terms. For in its course it points up some of the major, unresolved difficulties of the European radical tradition . . . The concepts 'nature' and 'biology' are not easy to deal with, particularly not in relation to sexual difference. Yet serious difficulties arise for feminists if these areas are positioned externally, as being outside of human culture.
>
> (Delmar, in Firestone 1979: 5)

This takes us back to the problems over sex and gender discussed in Chapter 1. Firestone's argument is that sexual difference does exist in the form of biological difference, but that this difference can be transformed through advances in reproductive technology. She argues forcefully against the idea that women have a duty or an innate desire to reproduce. Any female instinct for pregnancy is merely the product of the social construction of femininity and would be superfluous once human science had mastered reproduction. Firestone's utopia is one where sexual difference is eradicated: the difference in childbearing capacity is wiped out through the use of science, and the role of bringing up children, of 'mothering', is taken over equally by men and women in society.

This tendency to see reproduction as a site of oppression and to see motherhood as a burden from which women need to be freed is shared by other feminists, even if their solutions are not as extreme as those proposed by Firestone. These types of views, which were especially prevalent in the early years of second-wave feminism, meant that the focus of feminist thought and activity was on ways in which women could gain control of their bodies and prevent the burden of reproduction through the use of contraception and abortion. Early campaigns were fought over issues of widening access to safe methods of contraception and abortion to all women, and thus giving them the choice not to have babies. Less attention was thus paid to the processes of pregnancy and birth themselves, and to the conditions and state of motherhood. Ann Oakley (1986: 139) comments: 'As many people have pointed out, the women's movement articulated an implicitly, if not explicitly, negative evaluation of motherhood for many years before it was able to articulate the positive side.'

Some feminists have, however, articulated a very positive side to motherhood, and have argued that it can and should be a pleasurable and empowering experience for women. For these feminists, technology, rather than providing the solution to the burden of reproduction, often actually interferes in women's experience of pregnancy, birth and motherhood, and is used by men to try to take control of these processes away from women. Adrienne Rich (1976), for example, argues that it is medicine and technology, and specifically male control of that technology, that has made reproduction an area of oppression. This medicine and technology has been used by men because they are scared of women's powers of reproduction and motherhood, and want to control them. Male doctors and scientists have therefore written rules about being pregnant – what to eat and drink, how to exercise, and so on – and about giving birth. Doctors (largely male) have taken over control of birth itself from female midwives, and often use medical intervention with forceps, caesareans and so on, which reinforces their control of the birth and disempowers both mothers and midwives. Rich distinguishes between the social institution of motherhood, which has been the keystone of male control and oppression of women in diverse social and political situations, and the experience of motherhood, which can be both pleasurable and empowering for women. Part of the institution of motherhood that she criticizes is the ideology of the nuclear family, which has been instigated by men to ensure possession of their wives and children. A major problem for women is that the institution and the experience of motherhood do not match up, which means that often they find themselves alienated from their pregnancy, birth and motherhood. Women therefore need to reclaim their bodies and their motherhood for themselves:

> The repossession by women of our bodies will bring far more essential change to human society than the seizing of the means of production by workers. The female body has been both territory and machine, virgin wilderness to be exploited and assembly-line turning out life. We need to imagine a world in which every woman is the presiding genius of her own body. In such a world women will truly create new life, bringing forth not only children (if and as we choose) but the visions, and the thinking, necessary to sustain, console, and alter human existence – a new relationship to the universe. Sexuality, politics, intelligence, power, motherhood, work, community, intimacy will develop new meanings; thinking itself will be transformed. This is where we have to begin.
>
> (Rich 1976: 285)

Other feminists share Rich's concerns about male control of birth and motherhood, and have sought to try to document the history of this medicalization and its effects on women. Oakley (1986) argues that the result of medicalization and of the introduction of new reproductive technologies such as in-vitro fertilization and embryo transfer has been a preoccupation with 'physical cure' rather than 'psychological care':

> Thus we find in surveys of women's attitudes to prenatal surveillance the recurrent theme of a service provided by a series of strangers that is lacking in sensitivity to mothers' needs, marked by more of a respect for clinic routines than for the individuality of the patient, and so over-concerned with the possibility of biological pathology as to be oblivious of major psychological or social morbidity.

Motherhood, as a consequence, is caught between two paradigms: the scientism of medicine on the one hand, and pressure from feminism for women to be in charge of their own bodies on the other.

This debate over motherhood again raises questions in the context of the equality–difference debate. Feminists have shown a rightful concern about the way that the largely male medical profession controls women's bodies and have argued that women should take back control of their bodies and their experiences of motherhood for themselves. But in stressing the importance of motherhood for women, and in emphasizing aspects of love and care involved in this process, do we risk enclosing women once again in a state of difference – a state defined by their biological capacity to reproduce and their emotional capacity to mother? Is this not in part a return to the idea of women connected closely to nature, which feminists have sought to overthrow? As Michelle Stanworth (1990: 299) reminds us: 'The attempt to reclaim motherhood as a female accomplishment need not mean giving the natural priority over the technological – that pregnancy is natural and good, technology unnatural and bad.' This debate over motherhood has been made even more complex by the increasingly rapid development of new reproductive technologies, which could, it seems, realize Firestone's dream of removing the reproductive burden from women altogether. But is this a good thing? Many feminists have been rather wary of these new technologies, such as in-vitro fertilization and embryo transfer, and of the increasing legitimization and commercialization of the practice of surrogacy. They are seen as an extension of the medicalization of motherhood; a means for men, through the use of science, to gain even greater control over women's bodies.

Janice Raymond (1985: 12), for example, maintains that new reproductive technologies are a means for men to take away from women not only control of reproduction but reproduction itself. This point is supported by Gena Corea who, in her book *The Mother Machine* (1985), argues that because it is men who currently control these new reproductive technologies, they will be used to further men's control over women and to take the function of reproduction away from women. The new technologies, she maintains, involve splitting the functions of motherhood into smaller and smaller parts – donating eggs, 'growing' an embryo in the uterus, giving birth, bringing up a child. This splitting of motherhood into ever smaller parts leads to uncertainty about who the real mother of a child is and acts to reduce the power of women and their claim to their children. The new technologies are also accused of posing risks to women's health through the use of drugs and hormones to stimulate ovulation and so on, and of creating or increasing social pressures on infertile women to try to have children. Stanworth, however, argues against the wholesale rejection of reproductive technologies, arguing that under the right conditions some technology could be beneficial. In particular, she is critical of the division made between fertile and infertile women, arguing that although there are numerous social pressures that weigh on a woman's desire to have children, these pressures affect all women, fertile and infertile, and thus 'there is no particular reason to challenge the authenticity of the desire for motherhood of women who are infertile' (1990: 293). Stanworth claims that instead of merely dismissing all reproductive technologies out of hand, feminists should examine the different circumstances in which they are used and concentrate on trying to regain control of fertility for women.

One area of deep concern is over access not only to new reproductive technologies, but to all forms of fertility treatment and to contraception and abortion. Feminists have pointed to the ways in which some women are deemed suitable mothers and others are deemed unfit. These definitions depending on race, class, marital status, sexual orientation and so on have a clear impact on the ways in which doctors are likely to treat different women. Doctors and governments' views on control of fertility play an important role in determining women's reproductive choices and experiences (Dale and Foster 1986: 86). A white, middle-class, married woman is far more likely to be judged a suitable candidate for in-vitro fertilization, and doctors will be more likely to withhold this treatment from single, working-class women or women from ethnic minorities. Motherhood, it is clear, is perceived in a variety of ways, according to differences between women and between different societies. As well as doctors and governments making decisions about who is suitable to be a mother in their own countries, those from the developed countries have also attempted to control the fertility of women in the Third World through their advocacy of contraception and sterilization. Although this may take place in the context of international 'aid', these types of policies clearly imply value judgements about the value of motherhood in different countries.

The arguments among feminists over questions relating to reproduction and motherhood show that it is still a contested and difficult issue. One of the key problems is that, in attempting to regain control of motherhood for women, there is always the risk of falling into an essentializing division between women who can and do mother and men who do not. On the other hand, aiming to eradicate differences between men and women as far as reproduction and mothering are concerned may lead to something that could be a pleasurable and positive experience for women being taken away from them. For this debate to progress, feminists must, it seems, take account of the full range of reproductive and mothering experiences, including, for example, the forms of 'othermothering' (caring for children from the community who are not blood relatives), which, as Stanlie James (1993) points out, have been a source of empowerment for African-American women.

5

Ethnicity and Identity: The Problem of Essentialism and the Postmodern Challenge

A central theme of this book is that of the place of the notion of 'difference' in feminist thought. Although feminists have long pondered the question of 'difference' between men and women, the problem of 'difference' again rears its head in connection with the issue of divisions among women themselves – differences of race, class, ability and sexual orientation, among others. These types of differences and divisions have sometimes been ignored as feminists strove to describe an experience shared by all women and to identify common oppressions, and common strategies to overcome these oppressions. This search for communality, however, has led to the charge that some feminists have universalized from their own personal experience and have created an 'essential' model of woman – a model based on a dominant white, middle-class experience and aspirations. This universalizing and 'essentializing' approach has, critics argue, served to obscure the many differences such as those in racial, ethnic and class positioning that exist between women, and has thus in fact harmed some women rather than helping them. Although, as I have stressed throughout the book, there is not one feminism but a multiplicity of feminisms, and although these feminisms are the product of many different women in a variety of social positions, not all of these various feminisms have enjoyed the same prominence, and some feminists feel that the 'first-wave' and 'second-wave' feminist movements and theories were overly dominated by white, middle-class women who were theorizing and generalizing from the perspective of their own personal experience. This, it is claimed, has led to the experiences of many working-class and black women being overlooked. Moreover, it can also be argued that these first-wave and second-wave feminist theories were Eurocentric, basing their ideas and actions on the lives of white women in Europe and North America and ignoring or undervaluing the lives and experiences of women in the Third World, and the way in which these lives have been affected by the conditions of colonialism. Thus white, middle-class Western women were claiming to speak not only for all women in their societies but for women everywhere, universalizing from their own experiences and life situations and ignoring the effects of capitalism, racism and colonialism which proved divisive forces among women.

Black feminisms

One of the key challenges to the supposedly Eurocentric and essentialist nature of some feminisms has come from black feminists who have challenged white women's ability, and indeed their right, to speak for black women. A key black feminist theorist whose work has underlined this problem of feminism and racial difference is bell hooks, who, in her book *Ain't I a Woman* (1981), writes about the history of black women in the United States and their relationship to feminism. hooks argues that the rape and brutal assaults on black women during the period of slavery in the United States 'led to a devaluation of black womanhood that permeated the psyches of all Americans and shaped the social status of all black women once slavery ended' (1981: 52). Thus even now, a century after the abolition of slavery, US society still perceives and represents black women as 'fallen women', whores and prostitutes. The importance of this specific history of racial and sexual violence and the ways in which it has structured black women's lives and experiences in the

United States has not, however, been fully taken into account by white feminists, and hooks criticizes feminists, such as Susan Brownmiller (1975), who have written about rape and sexual violence but who have treated the rape of black women in the era of slavery as merely a result of the socio-historical context of the time, and have neglected to pay attention to the ongoing results of the period. As a consequence, such feminists neglect the ongoing sexist oppression of black women in the United States. The continuing sexual exploitation of black women and the devaluation of black womanhood during the post-slavery years was, hooks argues, part of a calculated method of social control designed to support white supremacy, but this was ignored by white feminists and, as the feminist movement began, there was little discussion of the way in which sexism and racism interacted to affect black women's position in society:

> If the white women who organized the contemporary movement towards feminism were at all remotely aware of racial politics in American history, they would have known that overcoming barriers that separate women from one another would entail confronting the reality of racism, and not just racism as a general evil in society but the race hatred they might harbour in their own psyches. Despite the predominance of patriarchal rule in American society, America was colonized on a racially imperialistic base and not on a sexually imperialistic base. No degree of patriarchal bonding between white male colonizers and Native American men overshadowed white racial imperialism. Racism took precedence over sexual alliances in both the white world's interaction with Native Americans and African Americans, just as racism overshadowed any bonding between black women and white women on the basis of sex.
>
> (hooks 1981: 122)

This claim by hooks that racism has taken precedence over sexism (even if she concedes that this is the case in the United States but may not be the case elsewhere in the world) implies serious problems for any feminist theories which attempt to treat women's oppression in a global fashion. For if the primary oppression is that of white over black and not that of women over men, then how can white women's and black women's oppression be theorized in the same manner? Even if, as other feminists suggest, racist and sexist discrimination are equally oppressive, then it is still difficult to conceive in what ways the interactions between the two types of oppression can be theorized and acted on in practical terms. This type of consideration clearly undermines any presupposition of women's sisterhood and challenges the assumptions of many white feminists. As hooks (1990: 29) argues: 'The vision of sisterhood evoked by women liberationists was based on the idea of common oppression – a false and corrupt platform disguising and mystifying the true nature of women's varied and complex social reality.' In fact it can be argued that along with racial differences, differences of ethnic and religious background, class, sexual orientation and so on all have an important impact on women's lived experiences and make it impossible to describe a universal and homogeneous oppression of women. However, these differences have all been ignored by some white feminists as they endeavoured to describe women's common experience and find a joint 'sisterhood'. As Audre Lorde (1984: 116), a black lesbian feminist, points out: 'By and large within the women's movement today, white women focus upon their oppression as women and ignore differences of race, sexual preference, class and age. There is a pretense to a homogeneity of experience covered by the word sisterhood that does not in fact exist.'

Thus hooks and Lorde, together with many other black feminist writers, have shown the ways in which white feminists have presumed a common oppression for all women, and because of this have overlooked ways in which black women suffer different oppressions. This also means that white feminists have sometimes ignored or misunderstood situations that can be liberating for black women. A good example of this misunderstanding can be found in some feminist analyses of the family. Many feminists have argued that the family is one of the major structures of patriarchal society and thus a prime site of women's oppression. Black feminists have argued, however, that although the family may be a site of sexist oppression for black women, it can also be a site of strength and resistance to racist oppression (Carby 1997). Furthermore, the feminist model of the family as a site of economic dependency for women may also prove to be false in the case of many black women, especially in societies where there is a high level of unemployment among black men. In these kinds of situation black women may find themselves as the chief income earner and the head of the family, with men economically dependent on them. Thus the family often has a different significance for black women, and any feminist theory that seeks to provide a universalized account of the family as a site of oppression will not necessarily apply to all women's situations.

Other feminist theories and campaigns have also ignored black women's specific experiences and struggles. Aziz (1997: 70) points, for example, to the feminist pro-abortion campaigns of the 1970s, which she argues:

> did not take into account the fact that many black women's reproductive struggles were around the right to keep and realize their fertility. For these women abortions, sterilizations and Depo Provera were all-too-easily available, and were often administered without adequate consultation and/or under the shadow of poverty.

Thus, what was for many white feminists a simple and universal demand for abortion, was in fact much more complex when placed in the context of the lives of black women. And it was only after the intervention of black feminists who exposed the false universalism of this campaign that future feminist campaigns around the issues of abortion and contraception were broadened to focus on choice in reproductive rights, including the choice for black women not to be forced into abortions or sterilizations without adequate consultation.

Not only are white feminists accused of a false universalism which hides women's different experiences and situations under the blanket concept of 'sisterhood', but, perhaps even more importantly, they are charged with failure to acknowledge their part in the racist structures of society. As Hazel Carby (1997: 46) argues:

> Black feminists have been, and are still, demanding that the existence of racism must be acknowledged as a structuring feature of our relationships with white women. Both white feminist theory and practice have to recognize that white women stand in a power relation as oppressors of black women. This compromises any feminist theory and practice founded on the notion of simple equality.

It does indeed seem to be the case that some white feminist theorists have ignored or undervalued the impact of racism, or else have distanced themselves from racism by claiming that this racism is part and parcel of patriarchal structures, of which all women, white and black, have equally fallen victim. And although other white feminists do acknowledge racism, they have argued that it is less 'fundamental' an oppression than sexism. This belief that sexism is the most fundamental oppression is shared by many of the classic texts of second-wave feminism. Kate Millett, for example, in her book *Sexual Politics*, seems to suggest that sexism is a more primary and more fundamental oppression than racism, as sexism is harder

to fight against, more pervasive and provides the 'most fundamental concept of power' in our societies (Millett 1970: 34). But, as
Elizabeth Spelman (1988: 118) points out, Millett herself describes
as an effect of racism the fact that black men do not have the same
authority over black women as white men do over all women, so
that her claim about the pervasiveness of sexism 'is belied by her
reference to the lack of authority of Black males'. This type of
feminist claim about the priority of sexism over racism, as well as
being theoretically unfounded, seems to ignore black women's
lived realities of racism and sexism, which are inextricably linked in
their everyday lives. Indeed it can be argued that black feminism
has demonstrated the impossibility of untangling race and gender
and shown that although dominant discourses may have tried to
separate them, the two are inextricably entwined. As Valerie Smith
(1990: 272) argues:

> Within dominant discourses, race and gender are treated as if they are
> mutually exclusive categories of experience. In contrast, black femin-
> ism presumes the 'intersectionality' of race and gender in the lives of
> black women, thereby rendering inapplicable to the lives of black
> women any 'single-axis' theory about racism or sexism.

Western and Third World feminism: Eurocentrism and colonialism

As well as ignoring or undervaluing racism in their own societies,
white feminists are also accused of Eurocentrism in their attitudes
towards women in the countries of the Third World, trying to
impose Western models of feminism sometimes inappropriate to
the particular conditions of women in these countries, and neglecting to analyse the ways in which colonialism and global capitalism
have shaped the experiences of women in countries outside Europe
and North America. One symptom of this Eurocentrism is an ignor-
ance of the endogenous roots of Third World feminism and a belief
that feminism originated only in North America and Europe and
that any other forms of feminist activity must be copies or imi-
tations of this original feminism. Kumari Jayawardena (1986), on
the other hand, argues forcefully that feminism was not a Western
creation but has endogenous roots in the Third World. As well as
challenging the belief that feminism was 'invented' in North America and Europe, she contests the views of some Third World writers
who have argued that feminism is a Western ideology not suited to

the conditions in their countries and that the fight for national liberation must come before that for women's emancipation. Jayawardena argues that in fact both these positions are erroneous and that feminism is not just an ideology imposed by the West on the Third World but has existed for just as long in Third World countries as in Western ones. As she points out, for example, there were already debates on women's rights in China in the eighteenth century, and movements in favour of women's emancipation in nineteenth-century India, so women in the Third World were already debating their social position and mobilizing to change at the same time as Western women were. This does not mean, however, that Western influence is not a factor in the development of feminism in the Third World. Western intervention has certainly played a role in creating the social conditions in the Third World in which feminism developed, with women's liberation movements almost always emerging in the context of nationalist struggles for independence from colonial powers. Jayawardena claims that 'struggles for women's emancipation were an essential and integral part of national resistance movements' (1986: 8), and women rarely organized autonomously but more usually as subsidiaries or wings of male-dominated nationalist groups. Similarly, the spread of capitalism was an important element shaping women's struggle for emancipation as the expansion of capitalism brought more women from their traditional roles in the home into the labour market outside the home and thus, in a way, facilitated feminist organizing.

Jayawardena thus highlights a fact that some Western feminists seem to have overlooked – namely, that women in Third World countries have developed their own endogenous feminist movements with their own specific goals. This point is also made forcefully by Uma Narayan, talking about the Indian feminist movement. Third World feminism, she argues, is a response to particular problems in Third World countries. And although anti-feminists in India have attempted to diminish feminism by branding it a Western import, the situation is that Indian women have specific problems which the Indian feminist movement has sought to address:

> Issues that feminist groups in India have politically engaged with include problems of dowry-murder and dowry-related harassment of women, police rape of women in custody; issues relating to women's poverty, health and reproduction; and issues of ecology and communalism that affect women's lives. Indian feminist political activities

clearly make feminists and feminism part of the national political land-
scape of many Third World countries. I am arguing that Third World
feminism is not a mindless mimicking of 'Western agendas' in one
clear and simple sense – that, for instance, Indian feminism is clearly a
response to issues specifically confronting many Indian women.

(Narayan 1997: 13)

While arguing for the autonomy and specificity of Third World
feminist movements, both Jayawardena and Narayan also highlight
the role of colonialism in shaping these movements. This Western
imperialism and its impact on women in colonized countries is
another area that is sometimes neglected in Eurocentric Western
feminist analyses, although some feminists, such as Cynthia Enloe
(1990), have paid close attention to the impact of colonialism on
women worldwide. Enloe argues that the relations between colonizers and colonized involved a particular form of gender relations
and gendered domination. Colonized women were represented in
ways that both eroticized and exoticized them, making them sex
objects for Western men:

Colonized women have served as sex objects for foreign men. Some
have married foreign men and thus facilitated alliances between foreign governments and companies and conquered peoples. Others
have worked as cooks and nannies for the wives of those foreign men.
They have bolstered white women's sense of moral superiority by
accepting their religious and social instruction. They have sustained
men in their communities when their masculine self-respect has been
battered by colonists' contempt and condescension. Women have
planted maize, yams and rice in small plots to support families so that
their husbands could be recruited to work miles away in foreign-
owned mines or plantations. Women as symbols, women as workers
and women as nurturers have been crucial to the entire colonial
undertaking.

(Enloe 1990: 44)

Moreover, representations of colonized women often served to
justify imperial domination as Western men pointed to women's
supposedly subservient and unemancipated positions in their own
countries and argued that they required the protection and civilizing influence of Western men. One example of this type of justification for colonialism was the issue of the veil or headscarf worn
by Muslim women, with many colonizing powers attempting to
'liberate' Muslim women by persuading or forcing them to remove
their veils. The French colonial powers in Algeria, for example,

undertook a campaign to try to persuade or force Algerian women to remove their veils.

This issue of the Muslim veil or headscarf is one that concerned not only colonial powers but also nationalist movements. Enloe (1990: 52) remarks that no practice has been more heatedly debated by nationalists than that of wearing the veil: should Muslim women support the nationalist cause by covering themselves with a veil or by taking off the veil and uncovering themselves? One of the aims of the colonial governments in Muslim countries was almost always to persuade or force women of those countries to remove their veils. They saw this as part of a 'civilizing' mission, and the more the women of a colonized country adopted Western dress, the more the colonizing power believed it had succeeded in its mission to assimilate the country to its Western, Judaeo-Christian values. This pressure from colonizers put Muslim women in a difficult position, making the veil a highly political issue and meaning that taking off the veil was seen as a statement of compliance or agreement with the colonizing power. This debate continues today, both with the rise of Islam in Iran, Afghanistan, Algeria and elsewhere, and in connection with immigrant Muslim populations in Western countries. It is an issue that is still proving difficult for Western feminists.

In France, for example, the exclusion of Muslim girls from schools on the grounds that their wearing of headscarves or veils contravenes the laws on secularism in education has split feminists, with some groups supporting the girls' right to wear their headscarves to school and others arguing in favour of a ban on the headscarves on the grounds that they are a symbol of the patriarchal oppression of Muslim women (Freedman in press). In supporting the ban on Muslim girls wearing headscarves in schools, French feminists subscribed to the Western views of Islam as patriarchal and oppressive of women and of French society as superior in this respect. They ignored the ways in which gender is constructed within a set of global power relations and, in asserting the superiority of French culture over patriarchal Muslim culture, many French feminists fell into the trap of ignoring their positioning as white women within a set of postcolonial power relations.

This type of issue highlights the ways in which Western feminists have been guilty of a Eurocentric approach that ignores the experiences and views of women from other countries and other cultures and imposes Western norms on these other women. Third World women are often seen as passive victims of patriarchal oppression, and their agency is ignored. Chandra Mohanty, for example, points out the way in which Western feminist discussions of issues such as genital mutilation, the Islamic family code, and so on, result in 'Third World' women being constructed as powerless victims (Mohanty *et al.* 1991: 57). If feminists are to avoid this Eurocentrism, they must be aware of the global postcolonial power relations within which they are operating. This is a complex issue, as Avtar Brah (1993: 201) points out: 'Our insertion into these global relations of power is realised through a myriad of economic, political and ideological processes.'

Gender and nation

These comments on feminism and global power relations point to a need for a gendered analysis of national projects and international relations. However, the political analysis of nations and nationalism is one of the areas of study that feminists have criticized for ignoring or undervaluing gender relations. Although women clearly have specific roles assigned to them in ethnic and national projects, theorists have often neglected these roles and have failed to analyse the differential integration of men and women in these national projects. Feminists have thus come to focus their attention on questions of gender and nation and on understanding the different contributions of women to nation-building projects. In their discussion of gender and nation, Nira Yuval-Davis and Floya Anthias point out that women are participants in ethnic and national processes in a number of specific ways (Yuval-Davis and Anthias 1989): as biological reproducers of the ethnic community; as reproducers of the boundaries of ethnic or national groups; as key actors in the transmission of the community's values; as markers of ethnic or national distinctiveness; and as active participants in national struggles. In all of these ways women have an input into national and ethnic projects that is distinct from that of men. Because of this, Yuval-Davis (1997) argues, one cannot properly understand either gender or nation without taking into consideration the ways in which the two are informed and constructed by each other. Such an understanding is necessary to the development of any international feminist politics as well as to adequate feminist analysis of issues such as immigration and racism.

The end of essentialism?

Challenges by black and Third World feminist writers have forced many white feminists to rethink their universalizing theories of women's common oppression and to acknowledge differences among women as a group. Acknowledging difference, however, is only one step towards deciding how best to promote a feminist agenda that will benefit all women and not just a privileged few. Debates continue, for example, about how best to theorize the interactions of racism and sexism and to combat both these oppressions at once, thus bringing justice to both black and white women. Moreover, the criticisms of black feminists who have uncovered a false universalism or essentialism in white feminist writing point to other types of differences among women, which must also be taken into account when feminists theorize social relations and try to build strategies to overcome oppressions and domination: differences of class, sexual orientation, age, ability and religion are only some of those that may have to be considered.

Having stated the importance of taking into account differences among women, there remains a clear problem about how feminists deal with these differences and how they should treat the interactions between different forms of oppression. Some have even gone so far as to suggest that this problem of dealing with difference undermines the entire feminist project and that since it is impossible to find a universal theory that applies to all women without essentializing what it is to be a woman, feminist theories are doomed from the outset. This leads to a serious dilemma for feminists today: should they continue in their attempts to use the collective identity 'women'; or should they abandon this attempt, which may seem doomed in the face of the difference problem, and merely theorize about specific groups of women and act on issues relevant to particular women in particular situations? Elizabeth Spelman (1988: 171) expresses this difficulty thus:

> Modern feminist theory is faced with a dilemma: will throwing out the bathwater of white middle-class privilege involve throwing out the baby of feminism? Moreover, though there are many versions of feminism (which vary according to the analysis of the nature of oppression, its causes, and what is necessary to end it), the dilemma applies to all versions – for all versions seem to rely on fundamental phrases such as 'as a woman'; on attempts to isolate gender from race and class; and on attempts to deal with race and class by adding the separate elements together to produce the sum of gender, race and

class identity. If we can't isolate gender from race or class, if we can't talk about the oppression women face as women, or about the experience of women as women, isn't feminism left without a foundation, without a specific focus?

In essence, what Spelman, in common with many other feminists, is asking is whether the charge of essentialism against a large part of feminist theory is one that is unanswerable and that can and will in fact paralyse the whole feminist project, leaving it without foundations. For, as I argued in the introduction, a base definition of feminism usually starts from the basis that it is about analysing women's oppression and trying to remedy it – if feminists cannot talk about 'women' as a group, will feminism have to disappear altogether?

Many feminists, however, believe that this charge of essentialism against them is overused and misplaced. And perhaps it could be argued that even if feminist theories can be accused of being essentialist, this does not really matter. One could even say that so-called essentialism is a precondition of any kind of normative political theory or indeed to any theory that intends to mobilize populations in order to effect social change. Socialist theorists, for example, talk about the working class as a group without necessarily identifying the multiple divergences in the working class; even liberal theorists, it can be argued, essentialize when they talk about the individual as a rational human being. This type of essentialism is necessary for social mobilization and can be a strategic tool to create group identity. And for those who find themselves in dominated or marginalized positions in society, the adoption of fixed or 'essentialized' identities can and does serve as an important strategic tool in their struggle against oppressions (Fuss 1989).

One potential answer to the feminist dilemma over difference and essentialism has come from poststructuralism and postmodernism. The impact of these theoretical movements on feminism will be explored in the next section.

Poststructuralist and postmodernist feminisms

Through an examination of black feminist critiques of some white feminist thought and the way it ignores difference, we have come to understand the difficulties in describing a common oppression of all women. These difficulties clearly relate back to one of the main themes of this book – namely, that of equality and difference and the problems that these two key concepts have posed for feminist theory and action. Critiques of essentialism in feminist thought have led to a debate over whether it is even possible or desirable to use 'women' as an analytical category. Some feminists have sought answers to these dilemmas and challenges in postmodern and post-structuralist theories which provide a set of alternative ways of addressing the problem of 'difference', and of approaching problems related to women's experiences and identities. These post-structuralist and postmodernist feminisms consider not only differences between men and women, or differences between women themselves, but also difference within and constitutive of the female subject or a difference 'within woman' (Evans 1995: 125). They reject the notion of a fixed female identity and in this way they believe that they overcome the problems of essentialism which other feminisms have had to face. For some feminists, this move away from fixed, knowable identities is a way forward that can overcome the seemingly neverending debate over equality and difference. For others, however, these poststructuralist and post-modernist viewpoints are actually damaging to the cause of feminism.

Poststructuralist and postmodernist feminisms are often discussed together as one group of theories, as if poststructuralist and postmodernist were interchangeable adjectives. As with other types of feminism, the labels postmodern or poststructuralist both cover a range of different theoretical and normative positions and it is thus difficult to make a clear division between the two. Moreover, it is clearly true that the two types of feminism do have many similarities and shared origins and approaches. So it may seem justified when academics writing about feminist theory decide to analyse postmodernist and poststructuralist feminisms as one (Evans 1995). Definition is made even harder in this case by the fact that postmodernism itself is a term that is notoriously difficult to define, as it encompasses a wide range of theories and positions. As Judith Butler (1992: 3) remarks:

> The question of postmodernism is surely a question, for is there, after all, something called postmodernism? Is it an historical characteriz-
> ation, a certain kind of theoretical position, and what does it mean for
> a term that has described a certain aesthetic practice now to apply to
> social theory and to feminist social and political theory in particular?
> Who are these postmodernists? Is this a name that one takes on for
> oneself, or is it more often a name that one is called if and when one

offers a critique of the subject, a discursive analysis, or questions the integrity or coherence of totalizing social descriptions?

In the same article, Butler argues cogently against tendencies to conflate postmodernism and poststructuralism and against an over-homogeneous use of the two terms (1992: 4). Other feminists have suggested that poststructuralism is perhaps an easier term than postmodernism to define, as the former may be linked with a some-what more restricted field of intellectual activity than the latter (Beasley 1999: 89). In this case poststructuralism may be under-stood either as an approach which is similar to but distinguishable from postmodernism, or as a 'subset' of postmodernism (Beasley 1999: 89). Clearly, however, the two approaches share a key set of features which will allow us to discuss them and their impact on feminism together.

Having pointed out such difficulties in describing postmodernism and poststructuralism, we must then go on to ask what relevance these approaches might have for feminism?

Some feminists, such as Jane Flax (1990), have argued that feminist theory is necessarily postmodern in that it challenges the natural, fixed and universal definitions of gender relations. Simi-larly, Patricia Waugh (1998) points out that if one takes post-modernism to entail a critique of ideas emanating from the Enlightenment, then one can argue that feminism has always con-tributed to such a critique of Enlightenment, arguing as it does that the notion of a universal, rational subject is inherently masculine, as is any understanding of history as one grand narrative of progress. Also, feminist theories of knowledge have rejected the idea that knowledge is an objective reflection of any independently existing world outside (Waugh 1998: 177). Having said this, however, postmodernist and poststructuralist feminists have criti-cized other feminists for rejecting patriarchal definitions of femi-ninity and masculinity but then constructing new fixed meanings of their own, so in their definition by no means all types of femin-ism are postmodern. In this respect, Linda Alcoff (1988) criticizes feminists such as Mary Daly and Adrienne Rich, who, she says, have adopted a 'cultural feminism' – a feminism that reappropri-ates the ideology of a female nature or female essence in an effort to revalidate undervalued female attributes. Chris Weedon, a post-structuralist feminist, is also critical of this type of reappropriation, as she argues:

Some feminist discourse has sought to offer alternative models of femininity by creating alternative discourses . . . In each case an alternative version of the truth of femininity is proposed, guaranteed by an
alternative source of meaning. The fixing of meaning is necessary for
social life but in allying meaning to true essential non-patriarchal femininity, such discourse inevitably attempts to fix femininity once and
for all. A post-structuralist feminism, on the other hand, committed as
it is to the principle of difference and deferral, never fixes meaning
once and for all. For poststructuralism femininity and masculinity are
constantly in process and subjectivity, which most discourses seek to
fix, is constantly subject to dispersal.

(1987: 99)

This is perhaps the vital contribution of poststructuralism and postmodernism to feminism: the challenge to the notion of a fixed definition of femininity and an undermining of the categories of woman
and man, masculine and feminine. Language is a central element in
this work of deconstruction of fixed analytical categories and identities, and poststructuralists and postmodernists work particularly
with the concept of discourse, which, as Weedon explains, can help
to explain social structures and behaviours, and the operation of
power within society:

Through a concept of *discourse*, which is seen as a structuring principle
of society, in social institutions, modes of thought and individual subjectivity, feminist poststructuralism is able, in detailed, historically
specific analysis, to explain the working of power on behalf of specific
interests and to analyse the opportunities for resistance to it. It is a
theory which decentres the rational, self-present subject of humanism,
seeing subjectivity and consciousness, as socially produced in language
as a site of struggle and potential change. Language is not transparent
as in humanist discourse, it is not expressive of the 'real' world. Meanings do not exist prior to their articulation in language and language is
not an abstract system, but is always socially and historically located in
discourses. Discourses represent political interests and in consequence are constantly vying for status and power. The site of this
battle for power is the subjectivity of the individual and it is a battle in
which the individual is an active but not sovereign protagonist.

(Weedon 1987: 41, original emphasis)

Postmodernist and poststructuralist feminisms thus assume that
femininity and masculinity have no fixed or knowable meanings
and they argue for the need to deconstruct the processes whereby
certain qualities come to be defined as feminine or masculine. Central to this process of deconstruction is the analysis of the various

discourses that determine the discursive constitutions of individuals as subjects. These discourses are located in competing social institutions and processes and are continually competing with each other for the allegiance of individual agents. The nature of masculinity and of femininity is one of the key sites of the discursive struggle for the individual in a battle to fix meaning temporarily on behalf of particular power relations and social interests.

There are elements in the poststructuralist and postmodernist critique of some feminism that are clearly relevant, in particular the emphasis on the changing nature of masculinity and femininity and the error of seeing these as fixed and universal, and the questioning of individual subjectivity. However, poststructuralist and postmodernist feminisms have themselves been criticized for taking away some of the power (particularly the political power) of feminist analysis. Linda Alcoff, for example, argues that what she calls the 'nominalism' present in some postmodernist thought – the idea that the category 'woman' is a fiction – leads to negativity which cannot be used as a mobilizing force: 'You cannot mobilize a movement that is only and always against: you must have a positive alternative, a vision of a better future that can motivate people to sacrifice their time and energy towards its realization' (1988: 421). With its emphasis on deconstructing meaning, can poststructuralism or postmodernism provide any positive, constructive goals for feminists to aim for? A second criticism relates to the poststructuralist and postmodern view of power and, more specifically, the way in which power is represented as dispersed throughout society. Critics argue that this view of power neglects the social and particularly the economic context of power relations (Walby 1992).

Identity politics or transversal politics?

Poststructuralist and postmodernist feminists thus argue for the deconstruction of the fixed category of woman and criticize other types of feminism for their essentialism in trying to define women and femininity. This poststructuralist and postmodernist critique may seem appealing in the face of the dilemma over difference outlined above, and it is clear that most feminists take seriously the critique of any type of universalist 'meta-narrative' of women's oppression. But does this mean that it is necessary to abandon 'women' as a category of analysis and to move away from political struggles based on collective identity? Not necessarily. It is obviously vital that feminists take into account differences of all kinds between women and take seriously the challenge to the idea of women as a collective identity. But this does not mean that there can no longer be collective struggle. As we argued above, the adoption of collective identities can be vital for political struggle. What is important is that these identities do not become fixed and unchanging. One formulation that has attempted to get beyond the problem of difference and to propose a way in which feminists can mobilize collectively without neglecting differences between women, is the model of 'transversal politics'. As Nira Yuval-Davis (1997: 131) explains: 'In "transversal politics", perceived unity and homogeneity are replaced by dialogues which give recognition to the specific positionings of those who participate in them as well as to the "unfinished knowledge" that each such situated positioning can offer.' This is a politics of coalition where people recognize their differences but also their common objectives, and it is these common objectives that provide a group identity. I would argue that to continue to be a powerful political force and a force for change, feminism must assume some kind of collective identity of women, while at the same time acknowledging difference. This collective identity can be found in a common cause – namely, the struggle against all types of oppression. Although forms of oppression and domination vary with time and from society to society, it is possible to form an alliance against the various oppressions that exist and to overcome differences to reach this goal. Similarly, although the postmodern and poststructuralist critique has pointed to the errors of searching for overarching explanatory theories of domination and power inequality, I would argue that this does not mean that feminism should abandon its search for causality and that feminists must continue to try to explain the causes of power inequalities in our society in order to prevail against them.

Bibliography

Afshar, H. and Maynard, M. (eds) (1994) *The Dynamics of 'Race' and Gender: Some Feminist Interpretations*. London: Taylor & Francis.

Alcoff, L. (1988) Cultural feminism versus post-structuralism: the identity crisis in feminist theory, *Signs*, 13(3): 405 36.

Allen, J. (1990) Does feminism need a theory of the state?, in S. Watson (ed.) *Playing the State*. London: Verso.

Anthias, F. and Yuval-Davis, N. (1992) *Racialized Boundaries*. London: Routledge.

Aziz, R. (1997) Feminism and the challenge of racism: deviance or difference?, in H. S. Mirza (ed.) *Black British Feminism*. London: Routledge.

Bacchi, C. (1991) Pregnancy, the law and the meaning of equality, in E. Meehan and S. Sevenhuijsen (eds) *Equality Politics and Gender*. London: Sage.

Banks, O. (1981) *Faces of Feminism*. Oxford: Martin Robertson.

Barrett, M. (1980) *Women's Oppression Today*. London: Verso.

Barrett, M. and McIntosh, M. (1982) *The Anti-Social Family*. London: Verso.

Barrett, M. and Phillips, A. (eds) (1992) *Destabilizing Theory: Contemporary Feminist Debates*. Cambridge: Polity Press.

Beasley, C. (1999) *What is Feminism?* London: Sage.

Beechey, V. (1977) Some notes on female wage labour in capitalist production, *Capital and Class*, 3: 45–66.

Beechey, V. (1978) Women and production: a critical analysis of some sociological theories of women's work, in A. Kuhn and A. Wolpe (eds) *Feminism and Materialism*. London: Routledge and Kegan Paul.

Benhabib, S. (1988) The generalized and the concrete other, in S. Benhabib and D. Cornell (eds) *Feminism as Critique*. Minneapolis, MN: University of Minnesota Press.

Bock, G. and Thane, P. (eds) (1991) *Maternity and Gender Policies*. London: Routledge.

Borchorst, A. and Siim, B. (1987) Women and the advanced welfare state

– a new kind of patriarchal power?, in A. Showstack Sassoon (ed.) *Women and the State*. London: Hutchinson.

Brah, A. (1993) Difference, diversity, differentiation: processes of racialisation and gender, in J. Wrench and J. Solomos (eds) *Racism and Migration in Western Europe*. Oxford: Berg.

Brown, W. (1988) *Manhood and Politics*. Totowa, NJ: Rowman and Littlefield.

Brownmiller, S. (1975) *Against Our Will: Men, Women and Rape*. New York: Simon & Schuster.

Brydon, L. and Chant, S. (1989) *Women in the Third World*. Aldershot: Edward Elgar.

Bunch, C. (1986) Lesbians in revolt, in M. Pearsall (ed.) *Women and Values*. Belmont, CA: Wadsworth.

Butler, J. (1988) Variations on sex and gender: Beauvoir, Wittig and Foucault, in S. Benhabib and D. Cornell (eds) *Feminism as Critique*. Minneapolis, MN: University of Minnesota Press.

Butler, J. (1990) *Gender Trouble*. New York: Routledge.

Butler, J. (1992) Contingent foundations: feminism and the question of 'postmodernism', in J. Butler and J.W. Scott (eds) *Feminists Theorize the Political*. New York: Routledge.

Butler, J. (1993) *Bodies that Matter: On the Discursive Limits of 'Sex'*. New York: Routledge.

Califia, P. (1981) Feminism and sadomasochism, *Heresies*, 12: 30–4.

Carby, H.V. (1997) White woman listen! Black feminism and the boundaries of sisterhood, in H.S. Mirza (ed.) *Black British Feminism*. London: Routledge.

Chodorow, N. (1978) *The Reproduction of Mothering: Psychoanalysis and the Sociology of Gender*. Berkeley, CA: University of California Press.

Chodorow, N. (1989) *Feminism and Psychoanalytic Theory*. Cambridge: Polity Press.

Corea, G. (1985) *The Mother Machine: Reproductive Technologies from Artificial Insemination to Artificial Wombs*. New York: Harper and Row.

Corea, G. (ed.) (1985) *Man-Made Women*. London: Hutchinson.

Dahlerup, D. (1987) Confusing concepts – confusing reality: a theoretical discussion of the patriarchal state, in A. Showstack Sassoon (ed.) *Women and the State*. London: Hutchinson.

Dale, J. and Foster, P. (1986) *Feminists and State Welfare*. London: Routledge and Kegan Paul.

Dalla Costa, M. and James, S. (1972) *The Power of Women and the Subversion of the Community*. Bristol: Falling Wall Press.

Davis, A. (1981) *Women, Race and Class*. London: Women's Press.

De Beauvoir, S. (1949) *Le deuxième sexe*. Paris: Gallimard.

Delmar, R. (1986) What is Feminism?, in J. Mitchell and A. Oakley (eds) *What is Feminism?* Oxford: Blackwell.

Delphy, C. (1984) *Close to Home*. London: Hutchinson.
Delphy, C. (1996) Rethinking sex and gender, in D. Leonard and L. Adkins (eds) *Sex in Question: French Materialist Feminism*. London: Taylor & Francis.
Diamond, I. and Hartsock, N. (1998) Beyond interest in politics: a comment on Virginia Sapiro's 'When are interests interesting? The problem of political representation of women', in A. Phillips (ed.) *Feminism and Politics*. Oxford: Oxford University Press.
Dworkin, A. (1981) *Pornography: Men Possessing Women*. London: Women's Press.
Eisenstein, H. (1984) *Contemporary Feminist Thought*. London: George Allen & Unwin.
Eisenstein, H. and Jardine, A. (1988) *The Future of Difference*. New Brunswick, NJ: Rutgers University Press.
Eisenstein, Z. (1984) *Feminism and Sexual Equality*. New York: Monthly Review Press.
Elshtain, J.B. (1981) *Public Man, Private Woman: Women in Social and Political Thought*. Princeton, NJ: Princeton University Press.
Elshtain, J.B. (1983) On the 'family crisis', *Democracy*, 3(1): 137–9.
Enloe, C. (1983) *Does Khaki Become You? The Militarization of Women's Lives*. London: Pluto Press.
Enloe, C. (1990) *Bananas, Beaches and Bases: Making Feminist Sense of International Politics*. Berkeley, CA: University of California Press.
Evans, J. (1995) *Feminist Theory Today*. London: Sage.
Firestone, S. (1979) *The Dialectic of Sex*. London: Women's Press.
Flax, J. (1990) Postmodernism and gender in feminist theory, in L. Nicholson (ed.) *Feminism/Postmodernism*. New York: Routledge.
Fraisse, G. (1995) *Muse de la Raison: Démocratie et exclusion des femmes en France*. Paris: Gallimard.
Freedman, J. (1997) *Femmes politiques: mythes et symboles*. Paris: L'Harmattan.
Freedman, J. (in press) 'L'affaire des foulards': problems of defining a feminist anti racist strategy in French schools, in K. Bloc and F.W. Twine (eds) *Feminism and Anti-Racism: International Perspectives*. New York: New York University Press.
Fuss, D. (1989) *Essentially Speaking: Feminism, Nature and Difference*. London: Routledge.
Gardiner, F. (ed.) (1997) *Sex Equality Policy in Western Europe*. London: Routledge.
Gilligan, C. (1982) *In a Different Voice: Psychological Theory and Women's Development*. Cambridge, MA: Harvard University Press.
Griffin, S. (1981) *Pornography and Silence: Culture's Revenge against Women*. New York: Harper and Row.
Harding, S. (ed.) (1987) *Feminism and Methodology*. Bloomington, IN: Indiana University Press.

Hartmann, H. (1979) Capitalism, patriarchy and job segregation by sex, in Z. Eisenstein (ed.) *Capitalist Patriarchy*. New York: Monthly Review Press.

Hartmann, H. (1981) The unhappy marriage of Marxism and feminism: towards a more progressive union, in L. Sargent (ed.) *Women and Revolution*. London: Pluto Press.

Hedlund, G. (1988) Women's interests in local politics, in K.B. Jones and A.G. Jónasdóttir (eds) *The Political Interests of Gender*. London: Sage.

Hernes, H. (1987) Women and the welfare state: the transition from private to public dependence, in A. Showstack Sassoon (ed.) *Women and the State*. London: Hutchinson.

Hernes, H. (1988) The welfare state citizenship of Scandinavian women, in K.B. Jones and A.G. Jónasdóttir (eds) *The Political Interests of Gender*. London: Sage.

Hill Collins, P. (1990) *Black Feminist Thought: Knowledge, Consciousness and the Politics of Empowerment*. New York: Routledge.

Hills, J. (ed.) (1986) *Feminism and Political Theory*. London: Sage.

Hirsch, M. and Fox Keller, E. (eds) (1990) *Conflicts in Feminism*. New York: Routledge.

hooks, b. (1981) *Ain't I a Woman*. Boston, MA: South End Press.

hooks, b. (1984) *Feminist Theory: From Margin to Center*. Boston, MA: South End Press.

hooks, b. (1990) Sisterhood, political solidarity between women, in S. Gunew (ed.) *Feminist Knowledge: Critique and Construct*. London: Routledge.

Hurtig, M.-C. and Pichevin, M.-F. (1986) *La difference des sexes*. Paris: Tierce.

Jackson, S. and Scott, S. (1996) Introduction, in S. Jackson and S. Scott (eds) *Feminism and Sexuality*. Edinburgh: Edinburgh University Press.

Jaggar, A. (1983) *Feminist Politics and Human Nature*. Totowa, NJ: Rowman and Allanheld.

James, S.M. (1993) Mothering: a possible Black feminist link to social transformation, in S.M. James and A.P.A. Busia (eds) *Theorizing Black Feminisms*. London: Routledge.

Jayawardena, K. (ed.) (1986) *Feminism and Nationalism in the Third World*. London: Zed Press.

Jeffreys, S. (1990) *Anti-Climax: A Feminist Perspective of the Sexual Revolution*. London: Women's Press.

Jeffreys, S. (1993) *The Lesbian Heresy: A Feminist Perspective on the Lesbian Sexual Revolution*. Melbourne: Spinifex Press.

Jenson, J. and Sineau, M. (1995) *Mitterrand et les Françaises*. Paris: Presses de la Fondation Nationale des Sciences Politiques.

Jónasdóttir, A. (1988) On the concept of interest, women's interests, and the limitations of interest theory, in K.B. Jones and A.G. Jónasdóttir (eds) *The Political Interests of Gender*. London: Sage.

Kanter, R.M. (1977) *Men and Women of the Corporation*. New York: Basic Books.

Koedt, A. (1972) The myth of the vaginal orgasm, in A. Koedt, E. Levine and A. Rapone (eds) *Radical Feminism*. New York: Quadrangle.

Landes, J.B. (ed.) (1998) *Feminism: The Public and the Private*. Oxford: Oxford University Press.

Laqueur, T. (1990) *Making Sex: Body and Gender from the Greeks to Freud*. Cambridge, MA: Harvard University Press.

Lewis, J. (1986) Feminism and welfare, in J. Mitchell and A. Oakley (eds) *What is Feminism?* Oxford: Blackwell.

Lister, R. (1997) *Citizenship: Feminist Perspectives*. Basingstoke: Macmillan.

Lorde, A. (1984) *Sister Outside*. Trumansberg, NY: Crossing Press.

Lovenduski, J. (1986) *Women and European Politics: Contemporary Feminism and Public Policy*. Brighton: Harvester Wheatsheaf.

Lovenduski, J. and Norris, P. (eds) (1993) *Gender and Party Politics*. London: Sage.

Lovenduski, J. and Norris, P. (eds) (1996) *Women in Politics*. Oxford: Oxford University Press.

Mackinnon, C. (1982) Feminism, Marxism, method and the state: an agenda for theory, *Signs*, 7(3): 530–45.

Mackinnon, C. (1987) *Feminism Unmodified: Disclosures on Life and Law*. Cambridge, MA: Harvard University Press.

Mackinnon, C. (1989) *Toward a Feminist Theory of the State*. Cambridge, MA: Harvard University Press.

Marshall, T.H. (1950) *Citizenship and Social Class*. Cambridge: Cambridge University Press.

McIntosh, M. (1978) The state and the oppression of women, in A. Kuhn and A. Wolpe (eds) *Feminism and Materialism*. London: Routledge and Kegan Paul.

Meehan, E. and Sevenhuijsen, S. (eds) (1991) *Equality Politics and Gender*. London: Sage.

Mellor, M. (1996) Myths and realities, *New Left Review*, 217: 132–7.

Mies, M. (1986) *Patriarchy and Accumulation on a World Scale: Women in the International Division of Labour*. London: Zed Books.

Mies, M. and Shiva, V. (1993) *Ecofeminism*. London: Zed Books.

Millett, K. (1970) *Sexual Politics*. New York: Doubleday.

Minow, M. (1990) Adjudicating differences: conflicts among feminist lawyers, in M. Hirsch and E. Fox Keller (eds) *Conflicts in Feminism*. New York: Routledge.

Mirza, H.S. (ed.) (1997) *Black British Feminism*. London: Routledge.

Mitchell, J. (1971) *Women's Estate*. London: Penguin.

Mitchell, J. (1975) *Psychoanalysis and Feminism*. London: Penguin.

Mitchell, J. and Oakley, A. (1986) *What is Feminism?* Oxford: Blackwell.

Mohanty, C. (1988) Under Western eyes: feminist scholarship and colonial discourses, *Feminist Review*, 30: 61–88.

Mohanty, C. (1992) Feminist encounters: locating the politics of experience, in M. Barrett and A. Phillips (eds) *Destabilizing Theory: Contemporary Feminist Debates*. Cambridge: Polity Press.

Mohanty, C., Russo, A. and Torres, L. (eds) (1991) *Third World Women and the Politics of Feminism*. Bloomington, IN: Indiana University Press.

Morgan, R. (1980) Theory and practice: pornography and rape, in L. Lederer (ed.) *Take Back the Night: Women on Pornography*. New York: William Morrow.

Mouffe, C. (ed.) (1992) *Dimensions of Radical Democracy*. London: Verso.

Narayan, U. (1997) *Dislocating Cultures: Identities, Traditions and Third World Feminism*. New York: Routledge.

Nye, A. (1989) *Feminist Theory and the Philosophies of Man*. New York: Routledge.

Oakley, A. (1972) *Sex, Gender and Society*. London: Temple Smith.

Oakley, A. (1986) Feminism, motherhood and medicine – who cares?, in J. Mitchell and A. Oakley (eds) *What is Feminism?* Oxford: Blackwell.

Oakley, A. (1997) A brief history of gender, in A. Oakley and J. Mitchell (eds) *Who's Afraid of Feminism?* London: Penguin.

Ogundipe-Leslie, M. (1993) African women, culture and another development, in S. M. James and A.P.A. Busia (eds) *Theorizing Black Feminisms*. London: Routledge.

Onlywomen (eds) (1981) *Love Your Enemy? The Debate Between Heterosexual Feminism and Political Lesbianism*. London: Onlywomen Press.

Ortner, S. (1998) Is Female to Male as Nature is to Culture?, in J.B. Landes (ed.) *Feminism: The Public and the Private*. Oxford: Oxford University Press.

Pateman, C. (1987) Feminist critiques of the public/private dichotomy, in A. Phillips (ed.) *Feminism and Equality*. Oxford: Blackwell.

Pateman, C. (1988) *The Sexual Contract*. Cambridge: Polity Press.

Peterson, V. S. and Runyan, A.S. (1993) *Global Gender Issues*. Boulder, CO: Westview Press.

Phillips, A. (1991) *Engendering Democracy*. Cambridge: Polity Press.

Phillips, A. (1993) *Democracy and Difference*. Cambridge: Polity Press.

Phillips, A. (1998) Democracy and representation: or, why should it matter who our representatives are?, in A. Phillips (ed.) *Feminism and Politics*. Oxford: Oxford University Press.

Raymond, J. (1985) Preface, in G. Corea (ed.) *Man-Made Women*. London: Hutchinson.

Reynolds, S. (1996) *France between the Wars: Gender and Politics*. London: Routledge.

Rich, A. (1976) *Of Woman Born: Motherhood as Experience and Institution*. New York: W.W. Norton.

Rich, A. (1980) Compulsory heterosexuality and lesbian existence, *Signs*, 5(4): 631–60.

Rich, A. (1986) *Blood, Bread and Poetry: Selected Prose 1979–1985*. New York: W.W. Norton.

Rowbotham, S. (1992) *Women in Movement: Feminism and Social Action*. New York: Routledge.

Sainsbury, D. (ed.) (1994) *Gendering Welfare States*. London: Sage.

Sapiro, V. (1998) When are interests interesting? The problem of political representation of women, in A. Phillips (ed.) *Feminism and Politics*. Oxford: Oxford University Press.

Scott, J.W. (1990) Deconstructing equality-versus-difference: or, the uses of poststructuralist theory for feminism, in M. Hirsch and E. Fox Keller (eds) *Conflicts in Feminism*. New York: Routledge.

Scott, J.W. (1996) *Only Paradoxes to Offer: French Feminists and the Rights of Man*. Cambridge, MA: Harvard University Press.

Segal, L. (1987) *Is the Future Female? Troubled Thoughts on Contemporary Feminism*. London: Virago.

Segal, L. (1999) *Why Feminism?* Cambridge: Polity Press.

Shiva, V. (1988) *Staying Alive: Women, Ecology and Development*. London: Zed Press.

Short, C. (1996) Women and the Labour Party, in J. Lovenduski and P. Norris (eds) *Women in Politics*. Oxford: Oxford University Press.

Showstack Sassoon, A. (ed.) (1987) *Women and the State*. London: Hutchinson.

Siim, B. (1988) Towards a feminist rethinking of the welfare state, in K.B. Jones and A.G. Jónasdóttir (eds) *The Political Interests of Gender*. London: Sage.

Siim, B. (1991) Welfare state, gender politics and equality policies: women's citizenship in the Scandinavian welfare states, in E. Meehan and S. Sevenhuijsen (eds) *Equality Politics and Gender*. London: Sage.

Siltanen, J. and Stanworth, M. (eds) (1984) *Women and the Public Sphere*. London: Hutchinson.

Smith, V. (1990) Split affinities: the case of interracial rape, in M. Hirsch and E. Fox Keller (eds) *Conflicts in Feminism*. New York: Routledge.

Snitow, A. (1990) A gender diary, in M. Hirsch and E. Fox Keller (eds) *Conflicts in Feminism*. New York: Routledge.

Spelman, E.V. (1988) *Inessential Woman: Problems of Exclusion in Feminist Thought*. Boston: Beacon Books.

Squires, J. (1999) *Gender in Political Theory*. Cambridge: Polity Press.

Stacey, M. and Price, M. (1981) *Women, Power and Politics*. London: Tavistock.

Stanko, E. (1988) Keeping women in and out of line: sexual harassment and occupational segregation, in S. Walby (ed.) *Gender Segregation at Work*. Milton Keynes: Open University Press.

Stanworth, M. (ed.) (1987) *Reproductive Technologies: Gender, Motherhood and Medicine*. Cambridge: Polity Press.

Stanworth, M. (1990) Birth pangs: conceptive technologies and the threat

100 *Feminism*

to motherhood, in M. Hirsch and E. Fox Keller (eds) *Conflicts in Feminism*. New York: Routledge.

Stoller, R. (1968) *Sex and Gender*. New York: Science House.

Tabet, P. (1998) *La construction sociale de l'inégalité des sexes*. Paris: L'Harmattan.

Tong, R. (1992) *Feminist Thought*. London: Routledge.

Tronto, J. (1993) *Moral boundaries*. New York: Routledge.

Viennot, E. (1984) Des stratégies et des femmes, *Nouvelles Questions Féministes*, 6–7: 155–63.

Viennot, E. (1994) Parité: les féministes entre défis politiques et révolution culturelle, *Nouvelles Questions Féministes*, 15(4): 68–83.

Vogel, U. (1988) Under permanent guardianship: women's condition under modern civil law, in K.B. Jones and A.G. Jónasdóttir (eds) *The Political Interests of Gender*. London: Sage.

Vogel, U. (1991) Is citizenship gender-specific?, in U. Vogel and M. Moran (eds) *The Frontiers of Citizenship*. Basingstoke: Macmillan.

Vogel, U. (1994) Marriage and the boundaries of citizenship, in B. Van Steenbergen (ed.) *The Condition of Citizenship*. London: Sage.

Walby, S. (1990) *Theorizing Patriarchy*. Oxford: Blackwell.

Walby, S. (1992) Post-post-modernism? Theorizing social complexity, in M. Barrett and A. Phillips (eds) *Destabilizing Theory: Contemporary Feminist Debates*. Cambridge: Polity Press.

Walby, S. (1997) *Gender Transformations*. London: Routledge.

Waugh, P. (1998) Postmodernism and feminism, in S. Jackson and J. Jones (eds) *Contemporary Feminist Theories*. New York: New York University Press.

Webster, P. (1981) Pornography and pleasure, *Heresies*, 12: 48–51.

Weedon, C. (1987) *Feminist Practice and Poststructuralist Theory*. Oxford: Blackwell.

Weedon, C. (1999) *Feminism, Theory and the Politics of Difference*. Oxford: Blackwell.

Williams, P.J. (1993) Disorder in the house: the new world order and the socioeconomic status of women, in S.M. James and A.P.A. Busia (eds) *Theorizing Black Feminism*. London: Routledge.

Wittig, M. (1992) *The Straight Mind*. Hemel Hempstead: Harvester Wheatsheaf.

Wittig, M. (1996) The category of sex, in D. Leonard and L. Adkins (eds) *Sex in Question: French Materialist Feminism?* London: Taylor & Francis.

Wollstonecraft, M. (1995) *The Vindication of the Rights of Women*. London: Everyman. (First published 1792.)

Young, I.M. (1990) *Justice and the Politics of Difference*. Princeton, NJ: Princeton University Press.

Yuval-Davis, N. and Anthias, F. (1989) *Women-Nation-State*. London: Macmillan.

Yuval-Davis, N. (1997) *Gender and Nation*. London: Sage.

Index

men
  black men, 79, 81
  male control of birth and
    motherhood, 71–2
  masculine culture in large
    corporations, 47
  and morality, 19
  and mothering, 22
  and pornography, 64, 65, 66
  rape and sexual violence, 64,
    66–8
  and unpaid domestic work, 52–3
  and women in paid employment,
    50
  and women's sexuality, 60, 61–2
Méricourt, Théroigne, 2
Mies, Maria, 54, 55–6, 57
Millett, Kate, *Sexual Politics*, 34,
  80–1
Minow, Martha, 65
Mitchell, Juliet, 49
Mohanty, C., 56, 85
morality
  and the equality–difference
    debate, 19–21
  and gender parity in politics,
    38
Morgan, Robin, 64
Morrison, Frances and James, 45
mothering, *see* reproduction and
    mothering
motherists, 11
multinational corporations, and
    the global economy, 54
Muslim women, and the veil,
    83–4

Narayan, Uma, 82–3
nations and nationalism, 85
nature
  and ecofeminism, 56–7
  and motherhood, 73
  and sexual difference, 10
Nye, A., 6

Oakley, Ann, 14, 16, 71, 72
  Sex, Gender and Society, 15

Ogundipe-Leslie, Molara, 58
orgasms, female, 61
Ortner, Sherry, 10

paid work, women in, 43, 44, 45–51
Pateman, C., 27, 29
patriarchy
  and radical feminism, 5
  and unpaid domestic work, 52–3
  and women in paid employment,
    48–51
peace movements, 3
Phillips, Anne, 37, 38, 39, 41
Pioneer, The, 45
political citizenship, 32–3, 42
political lesbianism, 61–2
political rights, 41, 42
politics, 4–5, 25–44
  'formal' and 'informal', 29,
    33–5
  of ideas and of presence, 38–41
  and the public–private
    distinction, 26–30
  and representation, 33, 35–8
  suffrage movement, 2, 4, 30–3, 39
  women and the welfare state, 30,
    42–4
  women's exclusion from, 25–6,
    28
pornography, 63–6
positive discrimination, and
    women's representation in
    politics, 36
postmodern and poststructuralist
    feminisms, 5, 7, 87–91, 92
  and deconstruction, 90–1
  defining, 88–9
  and the equality–difference
    debate, 8–9, 11, 12, 87–8
power relations
  and gender, 16–17, 18
  and politics, 34
  postcolonial, 84–5
  and postmodern and
    poststructuralist feminisms, 91
  in the private sphere, 28–9
  and sexuality, 60, 63, 64